THE SERVICE ADVANTAGE
HOW TO IDENTIFY AND FULFILL CUSTOMER NEEDS

Karl Albrecht
Lawrence J. Bradford

Dow Jones-Irwin
Homewood, Illinois 60430

Sponsoring editor: Jim Childs
Project editor: Lynne Basler
Production manager: Carma W. Fazio
Jacket design: Mike Finkelman
Compositor: Weimer Typesetting Company, Inc.
Typeface: 11/13 Century Schoolbook
Printer: R. R. Donnelley & Sons Company

Library of Congress Cataloging-in-Publication Data

Albrecht, Karl.

The service advantage: how to identify and fulfill customer needs /Karl Albrecht, Lawrence J. Bradford.

p.   cm.

ISBN 1-55623-247-0

1. Customer service. 2. Consumers—Research. I. Bradford, Lawrence J. II. Title.

HF5415.5.A43   1990

658.8'12–dc20

89–16953

CIP

Printed in the United States of America

1 2 3 4 5 6 7 8 9 0 DO 6 5 4 3 2 1 0 9

FOREWORD

by Jim Nordstrom

Nordstrom Department Stores

This book offers some excellent advice that all of us should read, reread, and diligently apply. It's about knowing who your customers are, what they want, and how they want to do business with you.

There is food for thought in this book for just about every type of service business I can think of, and even for those in so-called nonservice industries.

Karl Albrecht and Larry Bradford present a very eloquent case for sharpening your customer vision, and they have done a splendid job of rounding up the basic methods and techniques for doing that. They explain not only the "how" of customer perception research, but also the "why." And they explain how to discover the important keys to competitive advantage that lie hidden in customer research information. This is a very practical book and a much-needed contribution in an area where clear thinking and disciplined approaches are critically important.

Jim Nordstrom *is head of the highly successful Nordstrom department store chain, which, under his leadership, has become legendary for giving customers what they want.*

CONTENTS

1	**Know Your Customer**	**1**
	Who Knows Customers Better than Anyone Else?	2
	Who Makes a Fetish of Knowing Their Customers?	5
	The Employee Link	9
	The Customer as An Asset	12
	What Is a Customer?	14
	Thinking the Way the Customer Thinks	20
2	**Moments of Truth**	**24**
	Service Management	24
	The Service Triangle	26
	The Moment of Truth	30
	The Cycle of Service	33
	Critical Moments of Truth	35
	The Moment of Truth Model	36
	Special Moments of Truth	42
3	**Anatomy of the Service Customer of the 1990s**	**50**
	What Would the Lady Like to Drink?	51
	The 1990s Customer	52
	Service Products of the 1990s	66
	Service Contexts of the 1990s	71
	What Bugs Customers	78
	Who Will Be the Service Winners of the 1990s?	81
4	**The Customer Report Card: Blueprint for Excellence**	**83**
	What Is A Customer Report Card?	84
	The Customer Report Card Is Crucial to Business Success	87
	Discovering Your Customer Report Card	88
	A Sample Customer Report Card	90
5	**Customer Perception Research: Putting on Your Customers Glasses**	**95**
	What Are Demographics?	96

	Psychographics	99
	Research Methods	106
6	**Start with the Obvious**	**109**
	What's Going On Inside?	109
	The Employee: Your FrontLine Radar	110
	The Employee as Customer Advocate	112
	The Customer Is Always Telling You	113
	Customer Service Departments	116
	Management's Personal Radar	117
7	**The Face to Face Advantage**	**119**
	Interview Your Customers	119
	Depth Interviews	120
	Intercept Interviews	121
	Opportunity Interviews	123
	Telephone Interviews	124
	On-Site Interviews	125
	Focus Group Interviews	125
	Conducting the Focus Group Interviews	131
	Interpreting the Results	136
	Case: Accor	138
	Case: Santa Monica Hospital Medical Center	139
8	**Surveys: When, Why, and How**	**143**
	Planning the Survey Project	144
	Creating Your Questionnaire	148
	A Primer On Survey Statistics	159
	Processing Your Data	163
	Reporting Your Data	166
9	**Create Your Customer Report Card**	**171**
	Creating the Attribute Matrix	171
	Prioritizing the Attributes	179
	Selecting the Final Service Criteria	180
	Validating the Report Card	183
10	**Building A Service Quality Measurement System**	**186**
	Making Measurement a Habit	187
	Basic Structure for a SQMS	189
	Making Use of Informal Feedback	194
	Effectively Managing Customer Complaints	196
	Using Mystery Shoppers	204
	Producing Usable Reports	205
11	**Closing the Loop**	**208**
	Selling Better	208
	Delivering Better	216

Recovering Better from Mistakes   220
Building Better Systems   221
Attracting and Keeping Better Employees   223
Closing the Loop   230
Index   **233**

Recovering Better from Mistakes   220
Building Better Systems   221
Attracting and Keeping Better Employees   223
Closing the Loop   230
Index   **233**

CHAPTER 1

KNOW YOUR CUSTOMER

Your business success depends upon selling what the customer wants to buy.

And that knowledge, in turn, depends on knowing the customer's wants, needs, attitudes, and buying tendencies. Very few businesses have anything more than the most basic understanding of their customers' thinking. What's needed is a systematic approach that can put you in touch with your customers in such a way that your knowledge of them will create a competitive advantage for you in the marketplace.

The chapters ahead will lead you step-by-step toward superior customer knowledge. By getting good customer information and putting it to use, you'll be able to focus your business decisions more clearly when market opportunities present themselves. When you learn to look through the customers' glasses, you'll see new and different ways to launch campaigns, position products, and capture a greater share of your market.

Throughout this book you'll learn from the successes and mistakes of many other businesses, both in North America and abroad. The content applies especially well to the needs of small and medium-sized companies as well as large ones. The principles outlined ahead can be used effectively by all kinds of organizations, regardless of their business focus. You'll see how identifying and fulfilling customer needs has helped create a service advantage for utilities, hospitals, hotels, cruise lines, restaurants, banks, airlines, and retail stores, to name a few.

WHO KNOWS CUSTOMERS BETTER THAN ANYONE ELSE?

A good way to learn to do something better is to observe in action those who do it very well. It makes sense to study business operators who really know their customers in order to learn to be more customer-conscious. Probably those who know their customers better than anyone else are con artists, the masters of the "confidence games" from which they get their name. The scam artists. Society's leeches who like to prey on gullible "marks" with all sorts of tricks and schemes.

Why should we study these unscrupulous denizens of society's shadow regions in a primer for service businesses? Because there are a few important things we can learn from them. For all their cynicism and predatory behavior, there is probably no group that has focused more keenly on knowing their customers—intimately—than the con artists. Although they make their sordid living by fleecing unsuspecting victims, we can learn a great deal about the conduct of honest business by watching these experts of flimflam in action.

Come with us as we take a brief excursion into the world of the con artist. In 1988 an unusual film was released titled *House of Games*. The movie starred Lindsay Crouse in the role of a successful psychiatrist and author who became immersed in the murky underworld of the con men. Her guide was a character created by actor Joe Mantegna, who played a consummate con artist who was drawn to the curiosity and vulnerability of Crouse's character.

In one of the film's key scenes he shows Crouse (who has come to him to get a gambling debt forgiven for one of her patients) a glimpse of the con man's art. Intrigued, she watches as he demonstrates the simple trick of consistently guessing in which hand she has hidden a quarter. He can always guess correctly, he says, because she always points her nose just a bit toward the hand holding the coin. This, he explains, is a "give", short for "give-away", a sure-fire method for always winning the bet. Crouse decides to make a scientific study of the con men and their "House of Games", a move which nearly gets her killed as she switches back and forth from researcher to participant in the con games.

What Crouse discovers, and what real-life con men know, is that to be a successful scam artist, one must know his or her "mark," the intended victim, intimately. Those who would make us the victims of their clever games constantly study us, the average consumer, to learn what intrigues and motivates us, what turns us on, what our secret desires may be.

One of the oldest con games in existence, "Three Card Monte," is still going strong. It has succeeded over the years because the con artist knows that everyone wants to get something for nothing. Here's how it works: the dealer usually sets up the scam on a city sidewalk with lots of pedestrian traffic. He uses the back of a briefcase or cardboard box for a working surface. He shows three cards, then places them facedown. He rotates the card positions several times. Seems simple enough. Pick the red queen from among the three facedown cards. First one player bets and wins, then another, and another. There seems to be no way to lose at this game. Soon a crowd gathers and people are eagerly thrusting their money at the dealer, wanting a chance to win like the others they've seen. But, of course, they don't. Before long, the only one with any money is the dealer, who will later give a cut to the "winners," who were audience plants and partners in the scam.

We don't want to belabor the point, but there is something inherently fascinating about watching people who would normally, in all probability, be very careful with their money, eagerly try to give it away to a total stranger.

What's going on here? How do the con men and the gambling casinos regularly collect millions of dollars annually from people? Why do people withdraw their life savings and give them to total strangers who promise to double or triple their value? Do the con artists and the casino operators know something we don't? The answer is a resounding, yes! *They know their customers*. Us. You and me. Con artists have done excellent market research, and they have a relatively sophisticated understanding of human psychology. They make use of a tremendous amount of practical "consumer research" that has been handed down and passed along among their number for many generations. They know we have an insatiable curiosity. They know that millions of us still believe you can have something for nothing. They know that many people, if not most, have a trace of larceny hiding just below the surface of their socially obedient exteriors. They know we all want money, and we'd all like to get it the easy way. They know each of us has dreamed of what we'd do if our proverbial ship came in. And they create the illusion of sails on the horizon with every scam they pull.

We're not suggesting for a moment that you endorse the values or methods of these hucksters. But, we can learn a valuable lesson by watching them operate: KNOW THY CUSTOMER!

It's Open Season on Customers

We've learned from the con artist the value of really *understanding* the customer, but of course we don't have to emulate the predatory attitude that is usually the con artist's downfall. There's a reason the con artists and their ilk are often described in predatory terms. In the same manner the hunter studies and tracks the behavior of his or her target, so do the con artists. It's as though there is open season, all year long, with any weapons permitted and no license required to bag as much game as possible. We can extend the hunting analogy to service businesses, leaving behind the predatory motif. If we want to "catch" customers, we have to attract them with something of value—something they want.

It may be open season on your customers, too. You were "hunting" when you "bagged" them. You attracted them to your business with some "lure" or "bait" that caught their attention. And all of your competitors can do the same thing. Kennametal, Inc., manufactures tungsten carbide cutting tools in its factories throughout the world. Quentin McKenna, president of the company, says, "We have no God-given right to our customers." You might think of your customers as an endangered species, yet one on which there is open season. And there are plenty of hunters and trappers out there looking for them.

We've taken you on a tour of the dark side of knowing your customer. Surely there must be a better way. Surely there are positive examples from business and industry in which knowing your customer is a science based upon inquiry and service, not a scam based upon iniquity and stupidity. And, fortunately, there are exemplary businesses and individuals who have made a fetish of knowing their customers.

WHO MAKES A FETISH OF KNOWING THEIR CUSTOMERS?

There are two very useful kinds of customer knowledge: (1) knowing customers generally in terms of their buying patterns and motivations and (2) knowing them as individuals because of the close, one-on-one interactions that employees have with them. Large businesses often must rely on more general customer information because of the numbers of customers and the complexity of their makeup. Small and medium-sized businesses can often get to know the customer more intimately by relying on salespersons and other front-line employees as a source of market information. Here are some examples of both types.

Nordstrom

The Nordstrom family has created a chain of retail stores that have become legendary for their superior customer service. How do they do it? By finding out everything they can about what customers want from a retail store. According to company president, Jim Nordstrom, "Our salespeople are expected to be the eyes and ears of the company. We want them always to be asking their customers what new products, styles, and variations they want to buy. In this company, when a salesperson says the customers are asking for such and such, that carries more weight than the opinions of the buyers."

They discovered that customers want a no-hassle return policy. They want a pleasant environment and personalized attention from sales associates. They want sales associates who can solve a problem on-the-spot without a lot of forms to fill out and approvals required. In short, Nordstrom has made a science of finding out what is on their customers' "report cards" and then delivering the report-card factors at a grade-A level time after time. What Nordstrom has discovered is that by making a fetish of knowing your customers you can create an unnaturally large market share or charge a higher price for your product. And Nordstrom competitors have felt the pressure.

State Bank of South Australia

State Bank of South Australia underwent a complete change in its competitive strategy and management philosophy as a result of a careful examination of the perceptions of its customers. Chief marketing manager Ron Dent says, "We looked carefully at the reasons our customers gave for moving their accounts to our bank from our competitors. We found most of our 'capture' accounts resulted from incidents where other banks had done things to anger their customers. We hadn't really done much to win them."

According to Dent, they found they were losing their own customers for the same reasons. "We identified certain critical events, certain moments of truth, which were associated with losing and gaining customers," Dent says. "We've now made significant changes in our training program for branch managers, so they can handle these critical moments of truth better."

Marriott Corporation

The Marriott Corporation is equally committed to customer awareness and the measurement of customer perception. "We spend something in the neighborhood of $10 million a year on market research," says J. Willard "Bill" Marriott, Jr., chairman of the company. "We believe it's absolutely essential to know the markets we're serving and what our customers want to buy."

Palais Royal

Palais Royal is a chain of upscale retail clothing stores in Texas. When the oil business crashed in the 1980s, the Texas economy took a nosedive. Houston was particularly hard-hit. A significant number of Palais Royal's most affluent customers had very high charge account balances from the oil boom days. Faced with the very real business need to clear these accounts, Palais Royal used its knowledge of the Texan's sense of honesty and fair play. The company notified some of their key customers with large outstanding accounts that they would set up payment programs that would allow the customers to pay their bills and clear their accounts at their convenience.

Jerry Ivie, vice president and controller of the company says, "Either you're serious about customer service or you're not. You give your customers what they ask for." When store customers complained that fitting-rooms were no longer attractive and comfortable, the store spent $100,000 refurbishing them. Each fitting-room was also equipped with a light outside the door so customers could signal the sales associate when they were ready to be measured for clothing alterations.

"Our biggest customer complaint was that our stores were too packed with goods," Ivie says. "Racks were too crammed with merchandise and it was hard for customers to get garments off the racks." In response to this complaint, Palais Royal set up a 20,000 square foot merchandise staging area to hold shipments until individual stores called for them, thus allowing fewer garments to be placed on racks and making it easier for customers to remove and replace them.

Palais Royal uses routine paper documents as a source of customer knowledge. During a two-week period twice a year, a brief questionnaire is printed on the back of charge slips. More than 70 percent of the store's merchandise payments are made on charge accounts. "We get a 95 percent return on our questionnaires when we use the charge slip," Ivie says.

The Mandarin Oriental Hotel

The Mandarin Oriental of San Francisco is one of the newest hotels in the Mandarin Oriental Hotel Group, headquartered in Hong Kong. The Asian hotel group is committed to bringing the finest Asian service standards to the United States. The Mandarin Oriental is located in the heart of San Francisco's financial district, where it occupies the top 11 floors of a 48-story twin office tower. Wolfgang Hultner, the hotel's general manager, says, "Bricks and mortar were not enough . . . what our guests really wanted was the same kind of service we give them in Asia."

The Mandarin has researched the prime factors on the luxury hotel guest's report card. One of the findings, according to Hultner, is that guests tend to be influenced by the amenities they find in the bathroom. "It's no secret that the guest spends a great deal of time in the bathroom," says Hultner. "If the guest has a pleasant experience in his or her bathroom, it usually sets the standard for the rest of the hotel."

The Mandarin Oriental's bathrooms are evidence that the hotel group has listened to its customers. Many of the bathrooms offer full-size windows above the bathtub that look down on the city. All of them are completely equipped and leave nothing to be desired. Each bathroom contains two bathrobes and an array of special soaps and shampoos.[1]

Motorola, Inc.

In 1988 President Ronald Reagan presented the first Malcolm Baldrige National Quality Awards. Of the 66 firms that applied for the awards, three were chosen for the honor. Motorola, Inc., was one of them. With $6.7 billion in sales in 1987, Motorola is a giant in the communications industry. Its products include pagers, semiconductors, and two-way radios. The company has 99,000 employees worldwide. The Chairman of Motorola, Robert Galvin, says that a big part of Motorola's secret of success is because, "We listen. Customers are able to tell us things like, 'You're a little hard to work with. If you'd be more willing to do this or more enthusiastic about something; we could do more with you.'"[2] What Motorola has done is to begin to pay attention to its customers and what they want, a lesson many industrial giants have yet to learn. In fact, one of the lessons to be learned about service is that the longer a business has been in existence, the more likely it is that it has lost sight of what is important to customers.

Techsonic Industries

Located in Eufala, Alabama, Techsonic Industries manufactures depth finders that help fishermen measure water depth and locate fish. In nine attempts to bring a new product to market, Techsonic failed nine times. In 1985 James Balkcom, chairman of the company, interviewed 25 groups of fishermen across the country and discovered they wanted a gauge that could be read in sunlight. "The customer literally developed the product for us," Balkcom says. Within a year of introducing the $250 Humminbird depth finder, Techsonic's sales tripled, totaling $80 million in 1988. The company now claims 40 percent of the depth finder market in the United States. Techsonic's new corporate motto is, "The quality of any product or service is what the customer says it is."[3]

Du Pont

As competition for customer loyalty increases, many industry giants are rediscovering the need to listen to their customers and to produce what the customer wants to buy. Du Pont chairman Richard E. Heckert says, "As the world becomes more and more competitive, you have to sharpen all your tools. Knowing what's on the customer's mind is the most important thing you can do."[4]

THE EMPLOYEE LINK

Although the previous examples focus on companies' efforts to get better information about their customers, there is another source that many businesses overlook: the frontline employee.

When employees are trained to become on-the-spot market researchers, your business gains a valuable up close and personal look at the customer. Employees who are trained and encouraged to listen closely to their customers not only generate higher customer satisfaction, they also increase the company's knowledge about changing customer needs. Some examples follow.

CitiCorp

The service strategy for CitiCorp is based on what customers insist is important to them. To carefully track their customers, CitiCorp makes a special effort to hire people who will listen carefully to the company's customers. Dinah Nemeroff, corporate director of customer affairs, says, "The needs are usually simple, but it is our responsibility to ensure that those needs are met in a competent and timely fashion by recruiting personnel who can meet those needs while working in an atmosphere in which all needs—customer and employee—are being met. All segments of the team must work toward the same goal or the ultimate boss—the customer—will not be served."[5]

The Fire House Car Wash

A very unusual automated car wash is located in Denver, Colorado. The owner, Dick Kates, is a Harvard MBA with a special fetish for knowing his customers. "We try to constantly remind ourselves of our goal: the best car wash, in the shortest period of time, in the most pleasant environment, safely," Kates says. By talking to hundreds of car owners, Kates discovered they wanted three things when they brought their cars to be washed: speed, a clean car, and courteous service. The Fire House Car Wash constantly stays in touch with its customers to bring the latest technological improvements to its business. "We visualize customers' perceptions of us and adapt accordingly," says Kates. When customers complained to employees that their front license plates were getting bent by a circulating brush that passed over the front of the car, a whole new piece of equipment was installed to eliminate the problem. The

Fire House people work quickly and courteously to deliver a top quality service product. Perhaps the best evidence of a commitment to staying close to the customer is a bright red telephone in the spotless waiting room with a prominent sign over it reading Hot Line To The Owner.

The Salesman Who Never Forgot

Tom Reed may have been the world's best clothing salesman. He worked for many years in a men's clothing store in the small oil-refinery city of El Dorado, Kansas. Tom was locally famous for never forgetting the birthdays and anniversaries of his customers. He maintained a massive card-filing system with a card for each customer he served. On the card were the vital statistics about the customer's clothing sizes and notes about the individual style preferences. Every time a customer visited the store, Tom would dig into his file box, pull out the customer's card and make any changes needed to keep the file current. He always made a note, too, of the person's birthday and anniversary, if married. Efforts to convince him to use a personal computer to store all his customer information were met with a polite, but firm, "No, thank you."

Tom's customers could always count on a telephone call or card on their special day. He would also send cards to his customers to announce a new product or garment line. Over the years, he sold fine men's clothing to sons, their fathers, and, in many cases, their grandfathers. Tom, who retired several years ago, is a textbook case of the power of the frontline employee as a one-to-one market researcher. He made a successful career by constantly doing his homework on his customers. And, at the same time, he helped his employer's store capture a large share of the local men's clothing market.

The Waitress Who Does Market Research

Claire Lucas is a young woman who waited tables at Pete's Coney Island restaurant, a famous local diner in Denver, Colorado until it closed in 1987 after Pete, the owner, died. She has gone on to work in other restaurants run by Pete's brothers. If there were such a thing as a doctorate in the psychology of the diner customer, Claire would have one. She is a professional who makes a fetish of knowing her customers and their preferences. She knows their names, stays up on what's happening with their families, and knows what they like to eat and how they want to be treated. Her constant attention to staying in close touch with her customers has made her something of a legend among professional waitresses.

Claire uses "spot" market research, that is, she uses her daily encounters with her customers to constantly gather information. She not only takes orders for food, but also monitors how her customers' tastes change and how they respond to different dishes served in the restaurant. She shows a personal interest in her customers, asking about the latest business endeavors and how things are going at work. And of course, as you might guess, Claire has a great following of loyal, repeat customers who want to sit in her serving station. Think of Claire as a one-person service business. By identifying and fulfilling her customers' needs, she increases the flow of traffic to her station and creates a higher cash flow in tips. In effect, she captures an unnatural share of her "market." And the repeat business she brings to the restaurant is an added bonus for Pete's brothers.

In each of the examples cited there is a common theme: a business or an individual has become totally focused on what the customer wants, and then created a level of service that meets or exceeds their customers' expectations. They have a certain degree of fanaticism when it comes to learning about their customers.

THE CUSTOMER AS AN ASSET

An important lesson to be learned about service management is that the quality of a product is viewed quite differently from the quality of service. While most organizations are very conscientious about managing the quality of their products, they often don't view service to the customer as a product itself.

With that perspective they fail to realize a critical truth: *the customer is your most valuable asset!*

Ask most business owners to name the assets of their manufacturing plant, retail store, or medical office and you'll get a recital of the tangible equipment, inventory, buildings, computers, and furniture. Rarely, it seems, do businesses include their customers as an asset. But ask Jan Carlzon, president of Scandinavian Airlines System (SAS), and you'll get a more provocative answer. "Look at our balance sheet," he says. "On the asset side you can see so-and-so many aircraft worth so-and-so many billions. But it's wrong—we are fooling ourselves. What we should put there is, 'Last year SAS carried so-and-so many happy passengers,' because that's the only asset we've got— people who are willing to come back and pay once again. We can have as many aircraft as we want, but if people don't want to fly with us it's worth nothing."

Just think for a moment how you manage the assets of your business. You create an inventory so you can keep track of them. You make certain these assets are protected with adequate insurance in case of loss. You check on them regularly to see that they are running properly, and you provide regular maintenance to keep them in good working condition. What if you viewed your customers as an asset? How could you keep track of them? How could you protect them, as a valuable part of your business, against loss? How could you check on them regularly to be certain that their needs are being met, and how could you provide regular maintenance to keep them in "proper working condition," in other words, to keep them satisfied so they'll return to your business again and again?

That's what it means to know your customer. Part of this knowledge is the realization that customers must be treated as valuable assets, along with all the tangible goods your business owns. Your "ownership" of your customers is only temporary. As we mentioned earlier, there is always a competitor who is interested in acquiring your customers. Case in point: John Barrier isn't a very impressive looking man. He wears dirty construction clothes and drives an old pickup truck. He had been doing business for over 30 years with the Old National Bank in Spokane, Washington. He made his usual stop at the bank, but when he asked to have his 60 cent parking ticket validated, the teller refused. "She said, 'You have to make a deposit,' " Barrier says. He asked to see the manager, who also refused to validate the 60 cent ticket. So after 30 years, John closed his account at Old National Bank and took his money—all $2 million of it—to Seafirst Bank.[6] Doesn't it make sense to treat this most valuable asset—your customer— with the same care and consideration with which you treat your other business assets?

WHAT IS A CUSTOMER?

The answer to that might seem like a "BFO"—a blinding flash of the obvious—but many businesses and professions fail to realize just what customers are and how they should be managed.

A disturbing trend among medical professionals is the re- luctance—and sometimes resistance—to regard the person they treat as a "customer." They refer to them by many names—guest, patient, client, member, "the cardiac in room 310"—all manner of labels except the one that counts most: *customer.* Why is this so?

It seems that medical professionals, and especially physi- cians, resist the notion of "customers" for two reasons: first, the medical practitioner, whether physician, nurse or technician, views the sick person as one who is to be treated and healed, not as one who is paying a lot of money for medical services; second, they resist viewing patients as customers because of some belief that doing so cheapens the practice of medicine and reduces it to a level that is undignified and unprofessional. "We're not McDonalds," said one incensed physician.

While these reasons are understandable, they are also part of the problem of the quality of service provided by hos- pitals, clinics, and health maintenance organizations. Because they haven't come to know their customers beyond the symp- toms the person is expressing, many medical professionals un- intentionally dehumanize their patients.

When physicians, nurses, and other medical professionals begin to recognize their patients as customers who pay a great deal of money for medical care, they can begin to get to know them better on both personal and professional levels. Until they do so, they will not have realized what a customer really is—someone who comes to you and buys your product or service and who expects quality of service as well as product quality in return for his or her investment.

Utility companies provide another example. Like the medical profession, the utility industry, in many cases, has not clearly defined its customer. To the utility, the customer is often no more than a number, a statistic to be tracked and measured as a source of revenue. Are we being too harsh? We don't think so. Many utility companies fail to identify exactly what a customer is and what he or she wants from the local utility business. Customers are often referred to as "ratepayers," a term that effectively reduces the customer to "one who pays rates," one who is sent a bill each month and who obediently pays an amount for electricity or gas service. When customers are depersonalized into ratepayers, they lose their individual identities and tend to be treated as numbers.

A national study of utility residential customers was conducted by the Edison Electric Institute (EEI), the research and information association for the nation's electric utilities. One of the key findings of the study was that today's utility customer has a very different view of service than that held by the utility companies. While most utilities define service in the context of *reliability,* that is, the production of electricity on a regular and dependable basis, the study revealed that a significant number of residential customers defined reliability as *evidence that the utility company had caring and concern for its customers and that it had their best interests at heart.* The EEI research further suggested that those utility companies who really listened and responded to their customers' concerns were less likely to experience strong resistance when it came time to file for rate increases with their respective public utilities commissions.

Do government agencies know what a customer is? A state governmental office recently surveyed its employees in an internal climate study. One of the employees complained that "the public" seemed to always arrive between 4:30 and 5:00 P.M., just before closing time. The employee was incensed that working people would come at a time that was convenient to them and not to the government agency.

The occasions when the taxpayer is treated as a real customer, with needs to be filled, are so few and far between in governmental agencies that they stand out by virtue of their rarity. A more likely scenario is the "take a number" syndrome. Some government agencies should change their sign from "take a number" to "be a number" because that is the way they treat their customers all too frequently—as a faceless number in a long day of faceless numbers. It's a case of being unwilling or unable to view the customer as a source of valuable information for improving the quality of government service. Citizens are not viewed as customers who pay taxes for the government services (there's an oxymoron) that they are supposed to receive. We've reached the point where we hesitate to work with governmental agencies who want to become service-driven because of the near-impossible task of changing bureaucratic systems.

You would think that most businesses would know what a customer is and how to treat him or her. The resort/vacation industry is a case in point. Most customers of the leisure industry are in a positive frame of mind when they begin to plan a vacation. But it only takes a few instances of being treated like a nonentity for the resort/vacation customers to lose interest and take their business elsewhere.

A case in point: a well-known ski resort, located on the western slope of the Rockies, in Colorado, made it downright difficult for vacationers to plan a ski trip. The customers had to place one call to the resort to get reservations, another call to get airplane reservations, another call to get a rental car, and yet another call if they wanted to arrange any additional tour packages at the resort. The resort unwittingly placed a number of inconvenient obstacles between itself and the customer.

Success in the ski business is often a statistical measure of "skier days," the number of skiers on the mountain on a given day of the season. Just viewing the customer as "skier" overlooks the many other ways in which the vacationers use the resort, for example, as customers of the retail stores in the area, users of rental automobiles, parents who need babysitters, and diners in the area's fine restaurants.

When a cruise line company lost sight of what its customers wanted when taking a cruise, market share began to slip. Although the company was a market leader in Caribbean cruises, it still followed a marketing campaign geared to a sybaritic lifestyle. While many people choose ocean cruising as a vacation, the vast majority of the vacation public does not. Research with customers revealed a surprising finding: people were very concerned about gaining unnecessary weight during a cruise, so opted for other vacation choices. Apparently the cruise line marketing people had lost sight of how to define a customer in the more health-conscious society of the 1980s.

Often, resorts seem determined to boggle the minds of their customers. Maps of the resort are often nonexistent or designed in such a way that you would have to be a cartographer to understand them. In many instances, it is left up to the customer to find his or her way around. There seems to be a prevailing attitude of, "You're here and you're on your own." It's no surprise that the new super-resorts such as the Westin Kauai on Kauai and the Hyatt Regency Waikoloa on Hawaii, are such a hit with resort customers. Superior accommodations matched with superior service and ease in finding one's way around the resort are making places like the Westin and the Hyatt Regency the resorts of the future. And the vacationing public is willing to pay a hefty room rate for the special attention.

One only has to experience an average day dealing with airlines to realize how far removed their concept of a customer is from reality. Here is a true example of seeing a person as an object, not as a customer.

A gate agent was engaged in a heated argument with an elderly gentleman whose wife had boarded their flight ahead of him. He was denied boarding, apparently because the gate agent had failed to issue two boarding passes. The flight was late and oversold. When the man asked to have his wife taken off the plane, the agent refused. In frustration, he asked for the agent's name. "I don't have one," was the snarled response, to which the elderly gentleman replied, "Yes you do, and it's b----!" The gate agent called the airport security police, who drove up on the tarmac, lights flashing. They rushed in, grabbing the old man, who tried to reason with them. Meanwhile, his wife's plane was slowly backing away from the jet ramp. Of course, it isn't logical or fair to indict an entire airline on the basis of its treatment of one customer. We cite this case as an example of a failure to adequately ask or answer the question, "What is a customer?" When customers are reduced to numbers in a computer and treated in a coldly logical manner, the business loses sight of its most valuable asset. The customer is a person with needs and concerns who, to be sure, is not always right, but who must always come first if a business is to distinguish itself by the quality of its service.

The following definition has been posted on the bulletin boards of numerous businesses over the years, but no one

---

WHAT IS A CUSTOMER?

A customer is the most important person in any business.

A customer is not dependent on us. We are dependent on him.

A customer is not an interruption of our work. He is the purpose of it.

A customer does us a favor when he comes in. We aren't doing him a favor by waiting on him.

A customer is an essential part of our business—not an outsider.

A customer is not just money in the cash register. He is a human being with feelings and deserves to be treated with respect.

A customer deserves the most courteous attention we can give him. He is the lifeblood of this and every business. He pays your salary.

Without him we would have to close our doors.

Don't ever forget it.

Author unknown.

seems to know the source or the author. Ann Landers printed it in her syndicated advice column several years ago and reprinted it in 1988. The author, whomever he or she may be, deserves recognition for an excellent answer to the question, "What is a customer?" Male pronouns were exclusively used in the original piece, and it is presented here in its original version to preserve the integrity of the unknown author's words.

Ask Gerald M. Thomas, general manager of the Newmarket Hilton in Canton, Ohio, for his perspective on hotel customers, and he'll likely point out a card which is placed in each guest room with the following message on it:

To Our Guests

In ancient times there was a prayer for *"The Stranger Within Our Gates."* Because the Newmarket Hilton is a *human* institution to *serve* people, and not solely a money-making organization, we hope that God will grant you peace and rest while you are under our roof.

May this room and this hotel be your "second" home. May those you love be near you in your thoughts and in your dreams. Even though we may not get to know you, we hope you will be as comfortable as if you were in your own home.

May the business that brought you our way prosper. May every call you make and every message you receive add to your joy. When you leave may your journey be safe.

We are all travelers. From birth till death we travel between the eternities. May these days be pleasant for you, profitable for society, helpful for those you meet, and a joy to those who know and love you best.

Gerald M. Thomas
General Manager

Viewing customers as human beings with families and personal concerns, not just a source of revenue, sets the Newmarket Hilton apart from the average traveler's hotel.

What answers would you and your employees give to the question, "What is a customer?" From what perspective do you view them? It's easy, sometimes, to lose sight of the customer as a reason for our existence. Some studies done in the medical community have suggested that nurses and physicians go so far as to view their patients as an enemy—another light on the nurse's call board, another stop the physician must make during rounds. Here is our answer to the question, "What is a customer?"

A customer is a human being. He or she comes in all sizes and in all colors. A customer is a child asking for help in reaching a toy on a tall shelf. A customer is an elderly man who has lost his way in a maze of hospital halls. A customer is a woman who does not speak English very well and who is trying to make her needs known in the only way she can. A customer is a coworker asking for your assistance so he or she can serve the paying public. Taxpayer, patient, client, member, ratepayer, guest, cardmember—all are synonyms for the most valuable asset a business has—the customer, who comes to you and pays money for your service or product. What is a customer? **A customer is the reason your business exists.**

THINKING THE WAY THE CUSTOMER THINKS

One of the most frequently quoted lines in literature comes from the Scottish poet, Robert Burns (1759-1796): "Oh, wad some power the giftie gie us/ To see oursel's as others see us." There is an important message in that line for any business which truly wants to know its customers. You have to get inside the head of the customer and see your business as he or she sees it, not as you see it or as you fantasize it to be.

Everyone knows the Golden Rule: "Do unto others as you would have them do unto you." George Bernard Shaw once remarked, "Do *not* do unto others as you would have them do unto you; their tastes may not be the same." Shaw's point is well taken. In a service context it's probably best to do unto others *as they would have themselves done unto!* In order to do that, you have to know how your customers want "to be done unto."

The Need for a Shared Frame of Reference

Creating a shared frame of reference is a well-known prerequisite for effective human communication. When two persons are interacting they may or may not share a common frame of reference, even if they share other similar characteristics.

A recent incident at Chicago's O'Hare Airport illustrates the result of failing to share a frame of reference. A customer at the ticket counter presented a ticket with insufficient fare to take him where he wanted to go. He became loud and abusive, swearing at the gate agent, insisting that his ticket was valid. The gate agent attempted to explain to the passenger that he could make the ticket valid by paying an additional $75. The customer insisted he had been told by the airline that the ticket was good for travel. The gate agent repeated that a boarding pass could not be issued on an insufficient fare. And so it went. Back and forth, each person attempting to persuade the other to accept a different position. They did not share a common frame of reference, therefore little progress could be made to settle the dispute.

Successful businesses excel at creating shared frames of reference. They make a concerted effort to view the company through their customers' eyes. Here's a brief exercise to illustrate the concept. As you read the following scene, imagine yourself looking through the lens of a camcorder, making a video tape:

You are driving, looking ahead through the rain streaked windshield, the wiper blades making a rhythmic swish-click, swish-click, as they clear the rain from the glass. You see a hospital driveway entrance ahead of you and turn the car in. You park the car and walk inside the hospital lobby, and the person at the reception desk glances up briefly, then returns to conversation with a friend. Finally, the receptionist says to you, in a flat voice, "Yes?" You say you need to see Dr. Young and are given directions to Dr. Young's office. The receptionist returns to the other conversation.

As you walk through the hospital, you see an array of bewildering equipment and laboratories. People pass you, looking straight ahead. You find Dr. Young's office and enter. You check in at the receptionist's desk and are told to take a seat and wait until your name is called. Thirty minutes later, a nurse looks out the doorway leading to the examining rooms and calls your last name, mispronouncing it, then disappears down the hall. You hurry to catch up, are shown to the examining room, and told to sit down and wait.

The doctor comes in and gives you a perfunctory greeting, getting right to the business of diagnosing your problem. The doctor leaves, and you are told to find your way to the radiology department for some X-rays. The signs on the wall contain a puzzling map that is color-coded with a well-worn "You are here" arrow. As you try to find your way through this maze you look for a friendly face to ask for directions, but everyone seems to rush past you, eyes straight ahead, as though you do not exist.

Finally you arrive at the radiology room and are told by a clerk to "take a number." You sit and wait. And wait. Finally, someone steps briefly into the waiting room and calls your last name, again mispronouncing it. The X-ray room is full of equipment, and you feel somewhat intimidated as your X-rays are made.

Your last stop after the radiology department is the pharmacy, where you join a winding line of people waiting to have prescriptions filled. After 20 minutes, it is finally your turn to approach the counter, where a pharmacy clerk grabs your prescription slip and tells you to sit down until your name is called, in about 30 minutes.

After 45 minutes, you collect your prescription and leave the hospital. You make your way back to your car, which is parked far from the hospital entrance because there were no parking places close in. They were all taken by employee and physician cars. You leave.

This isn't a fantasy. What you've just read happens all the time, every day. And it's not limited to medical facilities. You can substitute a bank, a restaurant, a car rental agency, a retail store, or any other kind of business. When you look through the customer's lens you see a different picture of your business. And you'll need to get that picture clearly in focus.

You will need to learn the tools and techniques that we've discovered are essential for getting a clear understanding of what's going on in your customers' heads when they come to do business with you. In short, if you want to create a service-driven business or organization, you must become an expert on your customers. You must develop a sixth sense about your customers—in a way, you have to become as dedicated to knowing your customers as the con artists are about knowing theirs—only in a positive way. You must make a fetish of knowing your customers' problems and perspectives and learn from those individuals and businesses who have done that before you. You need to create a view of your customers as your most valuable asset, one that must be nourished and maintained if you are to keep their loyalty. You have to come to a clear understanding of what a customer is, in the context of your own business. And, finally, you need to get inside the head of your customer so that you can see your business through his or her eyes. Then, and only then, will you be in a position to construct a competitive advantage based on perceived quality of service.

NOTES

1. Peter Greenberg, "Bay View Adds to Asian Flair," *The Denver Post,* November 20, 1988, pp. 1, 7.
2. Mark Memmott, "3 Firms Honored For Top Quality," *USA Today,* November 15, 1988, p. 9.
3. Patricia Sellers, "Getting Customers to Love You," *Fortune,* March 13, 1989, pp. 38, 39.
4. Ibid., p. 38.
5. James Fraze, "CEO's Stress Employee Link in Quality Service," *Resource/American Society for Personnel Administration,* January 1989, p. 6.
6. Elisa Tinsley, "Bank Gets $2M Lesson," *USA Today,* February 21, 1989, p. 1.

CHAPTER 2

MOMENTS OF TRUTH

By now, well over 200,000 people have read *Service America!*, the best-selling book written by Karl Albrecht and Ron Zemke that introduced the concept of service management to America. It has become required reading in some of the biggest companies in the world, such as the Sheraton Corporation, Chrysler, Marriott, Bank of Montreal, England's National Westminster Bank, and a host of others. The sequel, *At America's Service,* by Albrecht, has been equally successful. These first two books were written to introduce the concept of service management and its implementation techniques on a broad scale.

SERVICE MANAGEMENT

Service management is a total organizational approach to making superior service the driving force of your business. It is a *transformational concept,* a philosophy, a thought process, a set of values and attitudes, and—sooner or later—a set of methods. The most compelling reason to gain superior customer knowledge and to make service your driving force is to create differentiation from your competitors. Think of it this way. Your business can probably be matched, in most ways, by practically any competitor who sets his or her mind to it. If you build a beautiful building, so can they. If you offer a new line of products, so can they. If a company has achieved cost parity with competitors, new ways to increase profitability will have

to be found. If you're a reader of business publications you know that many companies use price reductions to gain a competitive edge. But Harvard Business School professor Michael Porter believes this approach is a mistake. "Cutting price is usually insanity if the competition can go as low as you can," says Porter. "You have to find a different competitive tack. Quality becomes central—and so do service and innovation."[1]

A recent survey, commissioned by *American Banker*, revealed that only 20 percent of the customers of financial institutions characterize the quality of service as "great." Leonard Berry, professor at Texas A&M University and director of its Center for Retailing Studies, responded to the study: "I think these numbers should be a real source of concern to bankers . . . Good isn't good enough in today's deregulated, 'everybody getting into everybody else's business' marketplace."[2]

One of the most potent ways to create market differentiation is by linking the quality of service with the quality of the product. This is where many businesses hit an apparent dilemma. Often they feel the pressure of meeting budgets and bottom lines. They begin to view the quality of service and the very real need for fiscal responsibility as an either-or situation. Figure 2–1, below, shows how a three-way pull can begin to exert itself. While acknowledging the need for both *quality of product* and *quality of service,* the two can be pulled by a third dimension, *cost containment.*

FIGURE 2–1
The Dimensional Choice Model

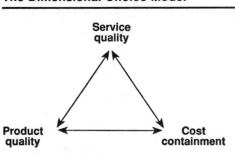

©1989 Lawrence J. Bradford

This model represents three important aspects of service management. It's surprising how many businesses entrap themselves into making a forced choice among the three elements. When a business sees each line of the model as an either-or dichotomy, feeling forced to choose between quality of service *or* cost containment; between product quality *or* service quality; or between product quality *or* cost containment, then options for intelligent business decisions become limited. What business owners and leaders must recognize is that you can create a *both-and* choice on each dimension. So you can have *both* service quality *and* product quality; *both* service quality *and* cost containment; *both* product quality *and* cost containment.

Service management creates a customer-centered organization that makes the customer's needs and expectations the central focus of the business. All aspects of your business, when service-managed, are structured to make it easy for the customer to do business with you. All interactions with your customers are governed by a single, inviolate principle: *the customer may not always be right, but the customer always comes first.*

THE SERVICE TRIANGLE

Just as service management has become the rallying cry for doing business in the 1990s, so has Karl Albrecht's Service Triangle© become the coat of arms for the flags of service managed companies, both nationally and internationally. The Service Triangle is a visual illustration of the whole service management philosophy, and we think it is important to reprint it here.

The parts of the service triangle are the Customer, the Service Strategy, the People and the Systems. Each of these key components is essential to a service-managed organization. This book focuses on the center circle, the Customer. Other books in the service management family will expand ideas for service strategies, training options, and system revisions. A brief introduction to the service triangle is in order.

FIGURE 2–2
The Service Triangle

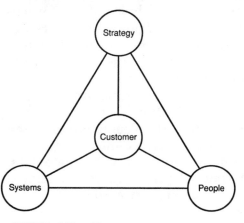

©1985 Karl Albrecht

The Customer

The heart of the model is the center circle, the Customer. By the time you finish this book, you'll understand a great deal more about getting to know your customers. Customers must be identified in both demographic and psychographic ways. In later chapters, you will learn how to discover both the demographic and psychographic characteristics of your customers.

The Service Strategy

Notice the line connecting the Customer circle to the Service Strategy circle. The service strategy is built upon the demographic and psychographic information you obtain in your quest to become intimately acquainted with your customers. It has two key parts: the official corporate commitment to service, which is internally focused, and the service promise to your customers, which is externally focused. The service strategy becomes a management model for future decisions about the company, its service, and its operations. This strategy, which must be based upon a clear understanding of the customer, is almost always hammered out by the ownership and senior management people in an executive retreat.

The People

This part of the service triangle model includes all the executives, managers, and employees in your organization. It represents the education aspect of service management. The line connecting this circle to the service strategy means that there must be a set of shared values about service throughout the organization. All persons must know, understand, and be committed to the service promise, which flows from the service strategy. Secondly, the line connecting the People circle to the Customer circle represents the face-to-face connection that all your company employees and managers have with customers. It also serves as a reminder that all people in your business must know what is on your customers' report cards.

The Systems

Please note the line connecting the People circle with the Systems circle. All persons in the organization, from top management to frontline employees, must work within the systems which organize how your business is run. Notice, too, the line from the Systems circle to the Customer circle. That is to show the interrelationship between your customers and your organization's systems. Your customers must work their way through your systems in order to do business with you. Finally, see the line that connects the Service Strategy circle to the Systems circle? Your service strategy will have a profound influence on your business systems as you gradually convert to a customer-focused organization. All organizations are composed of many systems that interlock. If you intervene in one of these systems, you affect all the other systems in the organization. But there are four major organizational systems, or subsystems, you will have to scrutinize if you want to create a service-drive culture.

The Management System.   If you are in a management role in your company, you are part of this system. Its members include the owners, executives, and managers who are actually in charge of the business and who make the strategic decisions that guide it on both short-term and long-term bases.

The Rules and Regulations System. These are all the guidelines for both employees and customers. These are the "laws" of the organization; what it's OK to do and what it is not OK to do. Example: employee handbooks, federal regulations, and management guidelines.

The Technical System. This system represents all the physical tools and techniques used to produce your product or service. For example, a hospital contains operating rooms, computers, file cabinets, telephones, surgical instruments, accounting systems, software, and the high degree of knowledge needed to practice medicine. All are part of the technical system.

The Social System. This is the human system. It represents all the people in the business and how they interact with one another; how they get work done together. This is the system in which people practice or do not practice teamwork, cooperation, problem-solving, and conflict management.

There are two key questions that must be asked about each of these major systems: (1) *Are they customer friendly?;* and (2) *Are they employee-friendly?* By "customer-friendly," we mean a system that makes it easy for the customer to do business with you. The second question turns attention inward to the organization. Are your systems "employee-friendly?" Are they set up in such a way that they make it easy for your employees to provide superior service to customers? Or do they, in effect, handcuff employees who really want to put your customers first, but are unable to because of some rule or regulation which they must follow?

In our work with service management, we have discovered that many systems have been designed and implemented for the convenience of the business and not for the convenience of the customer. When you stand back and look at your organization, do you see customer-friendly and employee-friendly systems?

This, in very brief form, is a basic overview of the service triangle. A fundamental understanding of it and the interrelationship of its components is essential for the work that lies ahead.

THE MOMENT OF TRUTH

This phrase, *the moment of truth,* has become the anthem for service management. The potency of the metaphor it suggests makes it not only descriptive but extremely useful for understanding the application of service management on a day-to-day basis.

Jan Carlzon, president of Scandinavian Airline Systems (SAS), used the phrase to rally the employees of SAS at a time when the airline system was in dire economic straits. He convinced them that every contact between a customer and any employee of the airline constituted a moment of truth. In these brief encounters, Carlzon argued, the customer made up his or her mind about the quality of service and the quality of product offered by SAS. Carlzon estimated there were 50,000 moments of truth in a given day in the SAS system; 50,000 moments of truth that had to be managed by every person, every hour, every day. His success in turning Scandinavian Airline Systems from near-bankruptcy to profitability in less than two years is a case study in service management. You can read the full, remarkable, story in Carlzon's book, *Moments of Truth.*

It is enough for now that you understand this: *a moment of truth is that precise instant when the customer comes into contact with any aspect of your business and, on the basis of that contact, forms an opinion about the quality of your service and, potentially, the quality of your product.* How many moments of truth are there in your business in a given day? Quentin McKenna, president of Kennametal, estimated that throughout the company's worldwide operations there is a contact with a customer for Kennametal every two seconds every day and that supporting this external contact are 60 events per second per day.

Your business may not have as many moments of truth as Kennametal or Scandinavian Airline Systems. But it's probably safe to say that there are several hundred that occur every day, and every one of them must be managed toward a positive outcome if you hope to renew your customers' loyalty time after time. It is important to remember that a moment of truth is not, by itself, positive or negative. It's how that precise encounter is managed that will turn the moment of truth into a positive or negative experience for the customer.

Also, keep in mind that a moment of truth doesn't necessarily have to involve human contact. The customer experiences a moment of truth when he or she drives into your parking lot. Are there sufficient parking spaces? Are the grounds clean and attractive? Is the entrance to your business easy to find? Are signs placed logically, and are they easy to read? All of these are potential moments of truth, and they happen even before you get a chance to perform for your customer.

You may have read about the man who unlocked his doors for business one morning. A number of customers approached his store entrance, seemed about to enter, then turned and walked away. All the lights were on in the store and it was clearly open for business. He checked to be sure the OPEN sign was facing out to the street. After observing quite a number of people come to the store's entrance, only to turn and leave, he walked outside his store to check the view from the customer's angle. Everything seemed fine until he tried to go back inside. That's when he discovered the door to his business would not swing inward as it should. He had to push very hard to get it open. A simple mechanical problem with the door had cost him potential customers. Every customer who approached his store and pushed on that unyielding door experienced a moment of truth and made an instant decision in his or her mind that the place was closed.

Of course, some businesses seem to want customers to go away. Consider this sign from a tire store: "If you're in such a hurry, maybe you'd better go away and come back when you have more time."

A former executive at a big steel producer told *Newsweek* reporters of the shock when a manager from Toyota arrived to inspect the quality of the company's sheet steel. The Toyota representative rejected sample after sample, saying, "No good, no good." "Our guys were furious," the executive said. "Instead of wanting to make the changes the Toyota guy wanted, they wanted to tell him where to go. So we lost the business."[3] Another moment of truth lost—and business lost with it.

The result of not managing moments of truth is that the quality of service, in the customer's eyes, regresses to mediocrity. And, just as often, that perception of mediocre service is transferred to the company's product line. Fair? No. Does it happen? All the time.

Barry Leeds, chairman of Barry Leeds & Associates, a research firm in the banking industry, estimates that only 28 to 30 percent of a bank's customers may be "extremely satisfied" with the service they get. "I consider the current level terrible," Leeds told a reporter for *American Banker.* "When we tell senior management that their banks fit within the norm, many of them are happy. I'd say they're happy with mediocrity."[4] One thing we've come to believe is that the pursuit of mediocrity is always successful.

How can you discover the moments of truth in your business? One way is to sit down with your managers, supervisors, and employees and brainstorm a list of the brief encounters your customers have with any aspect of your business. But you have to be willing to look through the eyes of your customers when you do this exercise. Don't try to rationalize or make excuses. Just list all the meeting points you can think of in which a customer forms a perception of the quality of your service and, potentially, your product. You should wind up with quite a lengthy list. That's just the beginning.

Fortunately, moments of truth don't happen in some random, brainstormed fashion. They usually occur in a rather logical and measurable sequence and that's good news for you, the business owner, executive, or manager. Placing the moments of truth in their logical sequence will allow you and your employees to identify those exact encounters for which they, as individuals, are responsible. The best way to accomplish this is to learn how to create a "cycle of service."

THE CYCLE OF SERVICE

A cycle of service is a map of the moments of truth as they are experienced by your customers. The cycle of service is activated every time a customer comes into contact with your business. Just as there are hundreds of moments of truth in a given business day, so are there many cycles of service.

The value of mapping cycles of service for the various aspects of your organization is that you are able to look through the customer's eyes and see your business from the customer's perspective.

Mapping out cycles of service is best done by the manager or supervisor and the employees who are directly involved in delivering service for that particular cycle. The technique is simple and effective. Using a flip chart pad or any large writing surface, you draw a circle. This will serve as the framework for listing the various moments of truth encountered by the customers as they experience them. It is important to list these moments of truth in their usual sequence, always being careful to view them from the customer's point of view. Figure 2–3 is an example of a cycle of service for a customer of a supermarket.

As you can see, there are many moments of truth in this shopper's cycle of service. The reason we suggest listing them in compass fashion on the circle is to stress to employees how every aspect of the customer's experience is related to every other aspect. Here's another way of looking at it. Managers and employees in most businesses tend to view their working day as a series of snapshots. If you were to supply each department with a camera and ask them to take a photograph of every person who comes to the department for help or to purchase a product, at the end of the day each department would have quite a collection of photographs. Some of them would be of colleagues, who are "internal" customers (more about that

FIGURE 2–3
The Cycle of Service Model

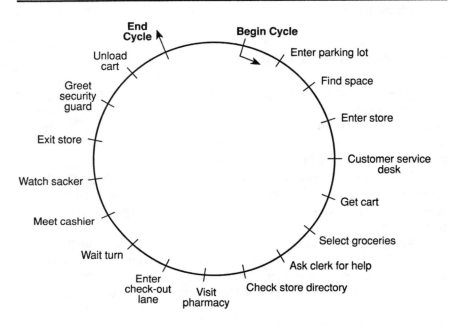

later). Others would be pictures of the many customers who passed through the department that day. The point is that people who provide products and services tend to see the interactions with their customers, both internal and external, as a series of discrete events that are not necessarily related to one another.

The customer sees the situation not as a series of snapshots, but as a movie, where every "scene" is connected to every other scene. By mapping out the service encounter the way we have in the illustration above, this point can be emphasized to those who have to manage the moments of truth in the cycle of service.

A second reason for illustrating service encounters in a cyclical fashion is to separate the important moments of truth from the critical moments of truth. While all of the moments of truth in a service encounter are important, there is usually a smaller number that are of such importance to the success of your business that they are called the *critical moments of truth*.

CRITICAL MOMENTS OF TRUTH

When you have created cycles of service for the major operations of your organization, you will be able to spot those moments of truth which, if not managed positively, will almost certainly lead to customer dissatisfaction, loss of loyalty to your service or product, and possible loss of the customer's business altogether. These are the critical moments of truth. It is imperative that persons in the organization whose work centers around these key encounters with customers be equipped with the skills needed to assure positive outcomes. For example, a critical moment of truth for most businesses happens when one of the organizational systems fails, as they certainly will from time to time. At that precise moment, the service reputation is at stake. When one of your systems fails it will take a quick-thinking person to make the situation right again with the customer. The "recovery record" for responding to systems failures is one of the hallmarks of credibility for the service-managed business.

Critical moments of truth vary, depending upon the nature of the business, the nature of the product, and the nature of the service provided to the customer. But one thing is common in all cases: the critical moments of truth, if left unmanaged, invariably lead to loss of customer confidence. Once you lose your customers' confidence, loss of loyalty and loss of repeat business quickly follow.

Another example of a critical moment of truth takes place daily in food service operations throughout the country. When you sit down in your favorite restaurant or in the company cafeteria, you peruse, in a semiconscious way, the cleanliness of the table, your dishes, and your eating utensils. Your perception of the temperature of the food, its taste, the correctness of the order, and the approach and courtesy of the serving person are all potentially critical moments of truth.

Take a second look at the cycle of service we created for the supermarket shopper in Figure 2–3. If you were the shopper in the example, which of these moments of truth would be critical to you? Some people value the speed of service at the checkout counter. So if they perceive the checkout counter is slow, the moment of truth has been lost. Lucky's, a chain of grocery stores on the West Coast, discovered this in a rather dramatic way. The company launched an advertising campaign which promised that whenever there were more than three people waiting in a checkout line, a new checkout lane would open. A minor customer rebellion broke out in one of the stores one day, when more than three customers were waiting in line and the new lane was not opened, as promised. Everyone in the line began chanting loudly, "Three, three, three!"

Others want a pleasant shopping environment. Another group wants people in the customer service booth to be helpful and courteous. While individual preferences will vary among customers, the critical moments of truth tend to be repetitive opportunities that cut across individual preferences. That's why it is absolutely essential that everyone in your business participate in mapping out of cycles of service for the various departments and divisions in which they work. It is the only way they can really spot those critical moments of truth where they have an opportunity to manage customers' perceptions.

THE MOMENT OF TRUTH MODEL

It's remarkable to see how many factors can go into a particular moment of truth. Each one can be unique in its own way. To be a service thinker means being able to understand and analyze the ingredients of any moment of truth, and to understand the factors that create quality at that instant. We have been developing more and more models and methods for analyzing this episodic quality of service.

A New Way of Looking at Moments of Truth

In *Service America!*, Karl introduced the Service Triangle©. The second book in the service management series, *At America's Service,* presented the Internal Service Triangle©. As we have worked with many managers throughout the United States and abroad, we've found an increasing number of people asking for a concrete model they can use to analyze moments

FIGURE 2–4
The Moment of Truth Model

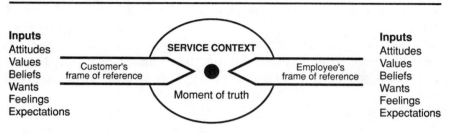

Inputs
Attitudes
Values
Beliefs
Wants
Feelings
Expectations

SERVICE CONTEXT

Customer's
frame of reference

Employee's
frame of reference

Moment of truth

Inputs
Attitudes
Values
Beliefs
Wants
Feelings
Expectations

©1989 Karl Albrecht and Lawrence J. Bradford.

of truth. In response to that need, we've evolved the model in Figure 2–4. It illustrates the rich diversity of the "inputs," that is, influencing factors, that go into any moment of truth.

It is a fundamental tenet of human communication that people assign meaning to the persons and events they encounter. An old saying among communication theorists is, "Words don't mean; people mean." The same principle applies to the moment of truth encounter in Figure 2–4. Let's take a closer look at this.

The Service Context

A major premise for explaining how we humans interact and communicate is that all communication is *context-bound*. That means that all the elements surrounding an interaction between two human beings have a profound effect upon the people, the interaction itself, and the outcome. For example, two persons discussing company policy face-to-face in a business office are in a different context from one in which they are talking about their personal relationship while curled up on a sofa in front of a fireplace.

Have you ever wondered why perfect strangers you meet on an airplane are willing to volunteer all kinds of personal information to you? It's because of the context: the airplane, the knowledge that your time together is limited by time and space, and the fact they'll probably never see you again. This phenomenon even has a name: "the bus-rider syndrome."

Now let's apply these communication facts to your business. All encounters between your customers and your business occur in what we call the *service context*. In the Moment of Truth Model in Figure 2–4, the service context, or setting, is the collective impact of all the social, physical, and psychological elements that happen during the moment of truth. Here's an example of an excellent service context that may surprise you.

The Santa Fe branch of the U.S. Postal Service in Denver has created quite a reputation for superior customer service. While "postal service" has been called an oxymoron by some people, this place is different. The clerks are friendly. They greet their customers and seem really eager to provide any help they can. On a recent busy morning, customers arrived to find a long line of people waiting to be served. One of the clerks working in the mail sorting room came out front to the counter and opened another window, "for any of you that need to do cash transactions." The service context that is created is the overall effect of the environment created by the attitude and approach of these clerks as they wait on customers.

Here's another case: car rental companies. There's a big difference in the service context when you check a car out as compared to the service context when you bring the car back to check it in.

When a rental car is checked out there is usually a big push to create added revenue for the rental company. Agents suggest a larger vehicle "for only two dollars more per day," or they try to sell expensive insurance "because you are responsible for the total cost of the vehicle in case of an accident." There are certain rituals and ceremonies connected with checking out the car: the presentation of the rental company's credit card, or some other major card; the validation of the driving license; the crediting of airline travel miles associated with some car rental firms; giving directions to your hotel or destination; riding to the rental lot in the rental car bus; and finally, being delivered to a shiny, clean (usually) late-model car. The keys are presented and you are invariably wished "a nice day."

But compare that service context to the check-in process. You arrive at the lot and park the car. A disembodied voice on a recorder booms out repeatedly, "Leave your keys in the car and proceed to the check-in desk." Here is a point at which the company and the customer perceive different service contexts from their respective frames of reference. The company considers the service complete when the bill is paid. To the customer, billing and check-in are a nuisance. The customer perceives that service is over when he or she gets out of the car. The rest is viewed as rigmarole for the company's benefit.

Rarely does anyone inquire whether the car was satisfactory or in good operating condition. No one asks if your business trip was successful, or if there is any additional service they can provide. There are no "value-added" ceremonies or rituals to make one remember the car rental firm as distinguished from any of the myriad others that are in business. In short, the customer walks away with a bill in hand and that's about it. There is no perceived benefit or value attached to the service context of turning in a rental car. The context is not one in which the customer feels valued. The check-in point seems to us to be an ideal moment to make a favorable last impression, but in our experience, this hasn't happened.

Here are some of the factors that contribute to the service context, which, when added to the inputs to the customer and service employee's frames of reference, have a powerful effect upon the moment of truth:

1. What is the environment, both physical and psychological, in which the service context occurs?
2. Does your service context create an environment in which the customer is predisposed to expect superior quality of service?
3. Does the service context created in your business say to customers, "Welcome! We're glad you're here!" or does it say, "Follow the rules and we'll get to you as soon as we can?"
4. Is the service context rigged for success or for failure? Is it set up and organized so that the customer invariably experiences satisfaction or frustration?
5. When systems fail, as they surely will from time to time, how do you recover in order to put the customer first?

6. Is the service context wedded to the computer system? Do your service employees know what to do if the computer system crashes?

Frames of Reference

Both the customer and the service employee approach the moment of truth encounter from their individual *frames of reference* which totally dominate their respective thinking processes, attitudes, feelings, and behavior at the moment of truth. The frame of reference acts as a filter and has a powerful effect upon the meaning which individuals in the service encounter assign to the moment of truth. Each person's frame of reference derives from many *inputs,* which are his or her personal attitudes, values, beliefs, wants, feelings, and expectations. Some of the inputs that create the frames of reference' may be automatic; for example, both persons may speak English, and both may represent social norms and customs with which they are mutually familiar. But some inputs to the customer's frame of reference may differ from inputs that create the service employee's frame of reference. When that happens, the two individuals view the moment of truth encounter from very different perspectives. It is also important to note that frames of reference can change in an instant. As the customer perceives that a need is being met or not being met, the frame of reference filter changes. Along with it, the customer's perception of the moment of truth changes. The same is true for the person who is providing the service or product for the customer.

Inputs to the Customer's Frame of Reference

Among the many possible inputs which help create the customer's frame of reference are:

1. Past experience with your business or businesses like yours.
2. Beliefs about what business you are in.
3. Expectations formed by their previous experiences.

4. Attitudes, beliefs, ethnic norms, and values that have formed during the customer's life.
5. Recommendations or warnings from other customers.

Inputs to the Service Employee's Frame of Reference

Among those inputs that help create the service employee's frame of reference are:

1. What the company has told the employee to do.
2. Rules and regulations set for service employees and customers.
3. The employee's level of emotional maturity.
4. Expectations of customer behavior based upon past experience.
5. Attitudes, beliefs, and values formed during the employee's life.
6. Tools and resources used to deliver your service or product.

Congruence

A key message of the Moment of Truth Model is the need for *congruence*, that is, a working compatibility among the three factors of context, customer frame of reference, and employee frame of reference. We noted earlier that if the inputs to the customer frame of reference and that of the service employee differ greatly, then the moment of truth may be adversely affected. Congruence means that there must be a meeting of the minds at the moment of truth. There must be some alignment of the customer's frame of reference with that of the service employee in order for the moment of truth to be won on a consistent basis. And both must be congruent with the service context. When there is a lack of congruence, the moment of truth is endangered.

You've seen it happen. Following a service problem, the customer describes his or her own actions as completely reasonable, rational, and polite. The service employee describes his or her own behavior in the same way. However, when the customer describes the behavior of the service employee, the employee's behavior is painted in terms of impatience, exasperation, and disrespect for the customer. The service employee, on the other hand, describes the customer's behavior as arrogant, demanding, and rude. The truth lies somewhere in between. But that's what happens when frames of reference become incongruent because of mismatched inputs.

SPECIAL MOMENTS OF TRUTH

Our work in service management has discovered new and revealing insights into customer behavior as related to moments of truth. It now appears that the moment of truth is the single most powerful element in the service equation. How the customer perceives the events and circumstances surrounding the moment of truth, that is, the context in which the service encounter occurs, and how the person delivering the moment of truth manages the interaction, determines the gain or loss of credibility of a business in the eyes of the customer. We believe the customer's decision to buy and to return to do more business is based upon several "special" moments of truth. These are particular encounters that are so decisive as to virtually predict the success of the entire cycle of service, and they deserve very special attention.

Buy/No Buy Moment of Truth

The next time you find yourself reaching for your wallet or checkbook, pause for a second and ask yourself what made you decide to buy that particular product or service? What was the exact point at which, in your own mind, you said to yourself, "O.K., let's do it?" This is the "buy/no buy" moment of truth. It occurs in every customer's mind as he or she ponders the decision to buy or not to buy. There is that one magical, mental instant when the customer says yes or no. We know that instant is influenced heavily by such factors as product display, interpersonal skills of the person dealing with the customer, the environment, the quality of the product, signs, and myriad other variables that have an impact on the customer during the moment of truth. There is also a psychological shift that takes place in the mind of the consumer when the decision to buy is made.

This is the fundamental difference between someone who is just looking and someone who is ready to buy. The just looking customer has not yet made the psychological commitment to purchase whatever it is your business offers. The ready to buy customer may have made this psychological shift before he or she ever entered your business. For example, compare two shoppers, one who is thinking about buying a new television set and one who is going to buy a new TV set but hasn't yet selected the store. Both are potential sales; however, the latter is poised, ready to purchase. This customer has already made the mental commitment to spend several hundred dollars for a television set. All that remains is to find a place where the psychological decision can be confirmed. The former has not yet made the psychological shift to the going to buy perspective.

If it's not careful, a business can create a service context which predisposes the customer toward a negative perception of the buy/no buy moment of truth. TicketMaster is a national company which sells tickets to traveling professional entertainment events. The company's policy is clearly illustrated at the ticket counter:

TICKETMASTER POLICY
CASH ONLY!
NO CHECKS
NO CREDIT CARDS
NO SEAT SELECTION ON
THE FIRST DAY OF EVENT SALES!

It sort of gives you a warm feeling all over, doesn't it? Even the name of this company, TicketMaster, carries an ominous tone. The impression one gets is that they are the "master," and you, the customer, are supposed to be the "obedient servant."

Here is a true incident which shows how the customer can be predisposed to view the "buy/no buy" moment of truth from a negative frame of reference. A man called TicketMaster so he could charge his tickets, then was told he would have to come to the ticket office to see where the seats were located (TicketMaster will not tell you your seat location by telephone). When he arrived at the ticket office he discovered he could not charge the tickets on his credit card at the office because of the TicketMaster policy stated above. Not surprisingly, no one mentioned this policy to him during his telephone conversation. While the service employee was very courteous and expressed sympathy, it didn't change the fact that the customer was inconvenienced. His only recourse was to drive to his bank, get the cash, then come back to the office and select and pay for his seats. A customer-unfriendly policy such as TicketMaster's is sometimes all it takes to help customers make up their minds not to do business with you.

Take a close look at your business. What are the buy/no buy moments of truth that need to be managed if you are going to attract and keep customers?

Value-for-Money Moment of Truth

There is a point at which every customer makes an assessment of value concerning your product or service. Even if you provide service that is clearly superior to that of your competitors, if what you are offering for sale in the marketplace doesn't meet the test of value-for-money, the customer won't buy. By the same token, having a wonderful product is not enough if the customer's frame of reference perceives a negative service experience when doing business with your firm.

This value-for-money moment of truth often occurs toward the end of the customer's mental gymnastics as he or she decides to buy or not to buy. After grading the service representative or salesperson on a mental report card, the customer comes to a fundamental choice: "Do I buy this product or service or don't I?" It can also come after the sale, when the customer drives off in the new car, or, for a medical patient, while healing from the surgery. The value-for-money moment of truth has an interesting impact on the buy/no buy moment of truth.

When you become a service managed business you have the opportunity to influence the customer at this point. The marriage between a top quality product and superior service is irresistible. One of the outcomes of being a service-driven business is that you may be able to command an unnatural share of your market. There may also be the opportunity to charge a higher price for your product. The value-for-money moment of truth is heavily influenced by both the quality of service and the quality of the product.

In a recent national conference for physicians, the doctors were asked to distinguish between quality of care and the quality of service. The ensuing discussion was a lively one. Most interesting was the fact that many of the physicians did not make a distinction between the two! The belief on the part of at least some of them was that if the doctor is competent and performs diagnoses and treatments which are technically correct, then the patient (we call them customers) will believe that a high quality of service has been established. In the debate which followed among the physicians, the prevailing view was that doctors treat value-for-money in the same context as fee-for-service. The word, "service," means the treatment performed by the physician. They agreed later that they weren't sure how their patients would define "service."

Repurchase Decision Moment of Truth

A special moment of truth which quickly follows the value-for-money moment of truth is the decision to buy again. Think of the last time you and a companion went out for lunch or dinner at a new restaurant neither of you had visited before. If the service context was a positive one, if the quality of the product—the food and drinks—was excellent, and if the service experience was pleasant, one of your first comments might be, "I'd go back there again!" It is at that point that an important piece of data is filed away in your brain. Even if the thought is not overtly expressed, you've subconsciously made a decision to repurchase the product or service sometime in the future. So the next time you and your friend are trying to decide upon a restaurant, you will remember the positive experience you had and the repurchase decision moment of truth will be reignited in your memory bank.

Even if you've somehow stumbled in your efforts to please the customer, you can still trigger a positive repurchase decision. Customers can be truly amazing. They seem to be anachronistic. They are at once the most demanding, selfish, and unreasonable people you'll ever deal with. Conversely, they can be very forgiving and understanding if they believe you are really trying to make things right.

How service employees recover when organizational systems fail can have a direct effect on the repurchase moment of truth. Credibility is gained, not lost, when your business can recover quickly and completely from some failure in your service system. Customer loyalty can actually be strengthened and enhanced when such recovery is carried out skillfully.

Referral Moment of Truth

The fact that most people will not tell you when they are dissatisfied with some aspect of your business is well known. Estimates are that up to 96 percent of unhappy customers won't ever complain directly—they'll just take their business elsewhere. But we know from our work in service management that while these folks may quietly slip away, they don't remain quiet for long. They tell others. You can count on at least 15 people, on the average, who will hear about the bad experiences your customer had in your business. This is a referral moment of truth. Do the same number of persons hear about it when the customer's experience is positive? Unfortunately, no. But that seems to be a fact of human nature. We tend to focus upon the negative more than upon the positive. When we find others who will share their war stories with us about poor service we can confirm in our own minds that our judgment in the situation was correct, so we have a chance to validate our own frame of reference. On the average, a satisfied customer will tell only a half-dozen other people or so.

The referral moment of truth is not one you can control or have an impact upon directly, because it happens, usually, in some place away from your business. But the moment of truth encounter will make a lasting impression in the mind of your customer and will trigger either a positive or negative referral at some later time.

Bad News Moment of Truth

There is a hilarious scene from the movie, *Planes, Trains and Automobiles,* which is a virtual documentary of service experiences in the travel industry. In the story, comedian Steve Martin is dropped off in the middle of a vast lot of rental cars, but when he finally reaches his car's space, there is no car. After walking a couple of miles back to the car rental place, he vents his frustration to the counter attendant who smiles sweetly throughout the tirade. In the pivotal scene, she asks nicely for his rental contract which he has torn up and thrown away in frustration. When he can't produce it, she delivers the "bad news moment of truth" with a smile of satisfaction that says it all: "Now I've got you, you S.O.B.!"

Why do some service employees seem to enjoy the bad news moment of truth? Probably for various reasons. Some employees may not be well-suited for service. Some have low self-esteem and feel hostile toward other people. Many service employees are, in fact, abused and vilified by irate customers whom, no matter how hard they try, they are unable to satisfy. So when it comes time to deliver the "bad news," they seem to take a perverse and special pleasure in the act. This is the old good-news/bad-news joke setup. The customer is about to have a negative experience as a result of something that may be completely beyond the control of the service employee.

We've seen bad news moments of truth that were handled about as skillfully as they can be under the circumstances. Experienced business travelers develop a finely tuned ear and can sense that we are about to experience a bad news moment of truth as soon as the gate agent begins speaking on the public address system.

These moments of truth are going to happen in any business, no matter how service-conscious it may be. It is the service context that is set, and how the bad news is delivered that will determine the response of the customer. Some of the bad news moments are extremely painful, for example, the physician who must inform a patient that the tumor is malignant. Such a moment calls for a special understanding of the customer's frame of reference and the inputs that are creating it at that very moment. The long-honored tradition of the bedside manner by the physician is never more crucial than when one of these life-threatening bad news moments must be managed.

Airline counter personnel vary widely in their abilities to handle bad news moments of truth. The most infuriating ones are those who choose to give out little or no information. Some are sympathetic and deliver the message in a skillful way. An apology, an expression of regret for the inconvenience caused by the malfunction or loss of luggage, can go a long way to creating the best possible outcome when a bad news moment of truth happens.

A key question to ask yourself is this: When the systems in your business fail in some way, and it is apparent that the customer is going to have to receive the bad news, how skillfully is it handled? How do your customers usually respond when one of these critical moments occurs? Do your service employees know how to handle an angry customer?

Perpetually Recurring Moment of Truth

Thousands of moments of truth may occur in your business daily. Some moments of truth occur for the customer on a perpetual basis, and you or your service employees may not be around to manage them. These are the "perpetually recurring moments of truth."

Every time you flip a switch to turn on the lights, that is a perpetually recurring moment of truth. Most of the time the lights go on. The reliability of electrical service in the United States is among the best in the world. But on that one occasion

when you flip the switch and nothing happens, you experience a momentary loss of confidence in the electrical company which supplies your power.

The driver of a car experiences a perpetually recurring moment of truth every time the key is inserted into the slot and turns on the ignition. Most of the time the car starts right up. But on that rare occasion when there is just a "click" and nothing else, the driver immediately feels a sense of alarm and concern.

The difficulty with managing the perpetually recurring moment of truth is that you or your employees are seldom around when it occurs, unless it happens in your place of business. It might be a good idea to make an inventory of all the perpetually recurring moments of truth that take place while your customer is on the premises. If you can identify them you can begin planning how you will recover on that day when the switch is flipped or when the key is turned and nothing happens.

NOTES

1. John McCormick and Bill Powell, "Management for the 1990s," *Newsweek,* April 25, 1988, p. 47.
2. Jay Rosenstein, "Bank Customers Serious about Service, Errors," *The Denver Post,* November 21, 1988, p. 3.
3. McCormick and Powell, *Newsweek.*
4. Rosenstein, *The Denver Post.*

CHAPTER 3

ANATOMY OF THE SERVICE CUSTOMER OF THE 1990s

We are in the midst of a basic shift from a world which manufactures, markets, and sells products, to one in which the customers demand the kind of product and service for which they are willing to pay. And if they can't get what they want, the way they want it, they will go somewhere else to find it. But many companies have not caught on yet. Many of them are still operating on the old paradigm value that they know what is best for their customers, and they haven't yet opened their ears to customer feedback. Western Digital Corporation (Digital) is a notable exception. When a new disc-drive controller board was produced at a cost of $150, one of Digital's major customers insisted on paying only $100 for each board. Digital's CEO, Roger Johnson, ordered the board to be redesigned to meet the customer's price. The result was a less expensive board that opened numerous other markets that had been previously untapped.[1] This willingness to listen to the customer and to identify and fulfill his or her needs and desires will become increasingly critical in the decade ahead.

If you want to maintain a service advantage for your business, you'll have to be sure that everyone who represents your organization has a solid understanding of the changing values of your customers. That's what this chapter is all about.

"WHAT WOULD THE LADY LIKE TO DRINK?"

The scene: an elegant restaurant. A woman and her male escort are shown to a table for dinner. The waiter gets into trouble right away. He speaks about the woman to the man, asking, "What would the lady like to drink?" as though she were not present. Then, he assumes that the woman is from the old school and wants the man to order for her; and finally, at the end of the meal, he presents the credit card slip to the man for payment, even though the woman uses her credit card to pay for dinner.

The waiter's frame of reference was created with inputs from values, attitudes, and beliefs of a time past. The female customer's frame of reference reflected inputs from a contemporary view of women and of herself as a professional businesswoman. Of course, how would the waiter know how to approach this particular moment of truth?

Without meaning to, service businesses can reflect values that cause unconscious discrimination. For all the progress that has been made in recent years concerning equal employment opportunity, women's rights, equality in the workplace, comparable value in job assessment, gay rights, and myriad other improvements, there are still those values that are carryovers from the 1950s and 1960s that can get in the way of dealing with today's customer.

Marilyn Taylor is vice president of human resources at Public Service Company of Colorado, the state's largest investor-owned utility company. Her training instructors are kept busy these days presenting courses in "pluralism." These courses help sensitize managers to differences in race, sex, and culture. Says Taylor, "Pluralism training has a high priority within our company given the anticipated makeup of our future workforce. All of the projections I have seen predict more diversity among workers. Preparing our managers to be able to more efficiently manage a diverse workforce only makes good business sense." She says many of the managers who go through the pluralism training are shocked, surprised, and sometimes angry when told that their behavior, in today's environment, is considered sexist, racist, or culturally insensitive. The company believes employees take their cues from managers and wants to make certain that both managers and frontline employees are sensitive to customers' differing value systems.

Those businesses that will survive will encourage much greater contact with their customers. They will realize that in a service economy a deeper and more complete understanding of customer attitudes, beliefs, and values is required than ever before. To gain a competitive edge by becoming service managed, you have to understand the anatomy of the customer of the 1990s.

THE 1990s CUSTOMER

A natural effect of the switch from a manufacturing-driven society to a service-driven one is the creation of various types of service customers. It's dangerous to use a "one size fits all" approach, hence the analysis in this chapter. Customers are more aware, more demanding, and more aggressive, than at any time in history. We are in the middle of a consumer revolution. Dorothy Phillips, president of Barnum Communications of Chicago, calls the new consumer a "take charger" who is highly self-centered.[2]

Attitudes, Beliefs, and Values

If you intend to gain a competitive edge with service management, you must understand the prevailing values, beliefs, and attitudes, and how they influence actions on the part of your customers.

Every customer who comes to your business carries certain mental baggage. Depending upon when they were born and reared—the generational type—certain attitudes, beliefs, and values drive their behavior. These deeply rooted elements represent the inputs that both your customers and your service employees bring into the moment of truth.

Claire Raines is a management consultant in Denver, who specializes in studying the baby boom generation—those folks born between 1946 and 1964. Raine's research has discovered that baby boomers are driven by the values of the 60s, a period that heavily influences their interpersonal and business relationships.

Whatever your values may be, they were formed early in your life. You learn to value honesty, fairness, the truth. As values are formed they create the things you believe in. From a fundamental value of honesty, you have the belief that it is wrong to cheat someone. From a value of fairness, you have the belief that people should be treated equitably. Attitudes are a reflection of the beliefs that we hold. If you hold a value of fairness and believe that people should be treated equitably, your attitude toward others will be geared toward sharing equally. And your behavior will likely be to divide what you have and to see to it that each person receives his or her fair share. As a negotiator, you will likely be one who likes to "find middle ground" and "split the difference." Compromise is probably your most successful way to manage conflicts. Values, beliefs, and attitudes are internal to each of us, and they are invisible to others. All that you can see in your customer is his or her external behavior.

When considering your customers' values, attitudes, and beliefs, it helps to understand their resistance to change. Values are, by far, the most resistant, because they are the building blocks of character. Raines says, "A baby boomer would no more consider changing from her sixties values than she would amputating one of her fingers." Second in resistance to change are customers' beliefs, the direct result of values. Customers' attitudes are easier to change than beliefs and values, and their behaviors are the easiest of all to influence.

A useful way to explore the values of 1990s customers is to view them as members of discrete generational groups. Each generational group has its own unique frame of reference, based upon the collective inputs peculiar to that group.

The Baby Busters

Your customers who were born after 1965 are members of the baby bust generation. The baby bust generation gets its name from the dramatic drop in birth rates after 1964, generally regarded as the end of the baby boom. These folks range in age up to 23 years old. By 1995 they will *represent 33 million of the American population.*

The Preteens

The younger members of this generation are subject to more parental influence in the purchasing of products than are those at the older end of the spectrum. They absorb a great deal of their product information from television advertising which is geared specifically to their tastes and age group. The younger the members of this generation are, the more likely it is that parents will make buying decisions for them. But the youngsters themselves can have a strong influence on their parents, using information gained from the media.

Tom Hanks starred in the movie *Big* in 1988. He played the role of a 12-year-old boy, whose wish to be "big" was granted. He was magically transferred to the body of a 30-year-old man. He soon discovered the need to make a living and landed a job with a toy manufacturer. In one of the most insightful scenes in the film, Hanks is discovered by the company president on a Saturday morning, his day off, playing with the many toys in the company's retail store. The president, realizing that his new employee understands toys from a child's perspective, makes the 30-year-old youngster the "Vice President for Product Development." The ability of Hanks' character to see the toy manufacturing business through the eyes of its primary customer—the child—is the heart of the film's success.

The youngest baby busters have been born into a world of electronic marvels which they pretty much take for granted. They like futuristic, electronic games and gadgets that are intriguing and challenging. They grew up pumping their quarters into video games, which are basically interactive computers, so they have little trouble transferring these skills to using personal computers.

The Teenagers

The teenagers in this group represent potent buying power. The Rand Youth Poll of 1984 estimated that 23 million teenagers in the U.S. have an annual income of $55 billion. Many young persons develop an entrepreneurial bent, looking for ways to earn money which can be converted into consumer goods. Through part-time jobs, babysitting, mowing lawns, delivering papers, and performing chores around the house, they accumulate their spending money. Some receive allowances from parents.

In 1983, the Rand Youth Poll profiled spending patterns for teenagers from 16 to 19. Both boys and girls in this group get about 60 percent of their spending from their own earnings and about 40 percent from allowances. Here is a breakdown (by percentages) of how they spent the money:[3]

Boys		Girls	
Savings	19.0	Clothing	24.4
Movies/entertainment	16.7	Cosmetics	18.8
Gasoline/car	15.9	Savings	17.0
Clothing	15.1	Gasoline/car	8.1
Food	12.3	Movies/entertainment	7.9
Personal grooming	6.5	Food	7.3
Hobbies	3.7	Hair care	5.4
Coin-operated games	3.6	Jewelry	3.8
Books/paperbacks	1.8	Records	2.7
Magazines	1.8	Books/paperbacks	2.0
Records	1.7	School supplies	1.6
School supplies	1.5	Coin-operated games	0.5
Cigarettes	0.4	Cigarettes	0.5
Total	100	Total	100

The Young Adults

They are between the ages of 18 and 25. Those at the upper end of the age range are on the cusp with the baby boomers, described below. According to the U.S. Bureau of Census, 42 percent of them are college students. Simmons College Market Survey estimates that 90 percent of college students are employed during their summer vacations and 60 percent work during the school year. Families of college students are generally affluent—47 percent of students come from families with incomes of $40,000 or more. These students represent a potential market estimated from $30 to $44 million. The nonstudents in this age group, of which the Census estimates there are 21 million, represent total income of over $100 billion.[4]

The Baby Boomers

More has been written and discussed about this generation than any other. You are a baby boomer if your birthday falls between 1946 and 1964. During that time, *96 million* of you were born.

Members of the baby boom generation are now between the ages of 25 and 43. They represent the single largest group of potential customers, one third of the entire U.S. population. Because of their size and buying power, we will place a good deal of emphasis upon understanding this generation from post-World War II and the 60s. Landon Y. Jones, in his book, *Great Expectations: America and the Baby Boom Generation,* called baby boomers the "New Breed of consumers that would best reward those who best understood them."[5]

This is one of the highest-educated groups in America. Over 18 million received college degrees between 1968, when the first baby boomers graduated, and 1987, according to the Department of Education's Center for Education Statistics.

The first wave of baby boomers, now aged 35 to 43, represents the biggest spenders among this generation. Claire Raines, author of *The Big Chill Generation At Work*™, says these customers are different from any before them. "Prior to the early 1960s most Americans were driven by the value systems of loyalty to country, their community, and their employer," says Raines. "They respected authority and believed in a world of law and order."[6]

With the Vietnam War came a clash between expectation and reality. The idealism of the 60s was in conflict with the reality of war. Those Americans who had fought in World War II and in Korea represented the loyalist value system. This contrasted sharply with the new value system of idealism forged in the Kennedy years.

A tremendous interest in the Vietnam War experience took place in the 70s and 80s. The theaters filled with audiences for movies such as *The Deer Hunter, Apocalypse Now, Coming Home, Platoon,* and *Full Metal Jacket,* many seeking to understand a war that made no sense to them.

They looked for ways to recapture their idealism. During the late 1980s, movies based on the values of the 50s and 60s became very popular. In 1985 Universal studios released *Back To The Future,* the 10th highest-grossing film ($104,237,346) of all time. It was a blockbuster hit, triggering a wave of nostalgia for life in the 50s and 60s that spilled over into television with shows such as "Thirtysomething" (Emmy for best drama series, 1988), and "The Wonder Years," (Emmy for best comedy series, 1988).

Six major values drive the baby boomers' behavior, according to Raines, and they will continue to do so in the 1990s:

Involvement

They were the protestors during the Vietnam War. They were the activists and they continue to be involved today. They were skeptical of authority then and they still are, to a certain extent, even as they pass into middle age. In a *Time* magazine survey, 55 percent of them expressed a distrust of the government and 64 percent expressed disloyalty to big corporations. Today's baby boomers retain their strong need for involvement and the belief that what they are doing is significant and will make a difference.

Pursuit of Self

They were the flower children. Their fascination with transcendental meditation, mind-expanding drugs, est, and eastern philosophy and religion was inner-directed. They were in a search for their identities. Today, they express the continuation of that search with a phenomenal interest in spiritualism, the New Age, using crystals for healing, self-help books, and personal development seminars. They spend millions of dollars annually in the quest for self-improvement.

Equality
They were the marchers for civil rights. They burned their bras and waged war on poverty. They went abroad to serve in Kennedy's citizen Peace Corps. The baby boomers are the first generation to grow up with racial integration and they have remained committed to equality. They actively promote gay rights and campaign for the homeless.

Nature
They were the "save the planet" generation. The "back to the earth" group avoided, as much as possible, anything artificially produced. The baby boomers of the early 60s focused instead upon natural products in clothing, food, and even medicine, putting great stock in herbal cures. They idealized an agrarian state where organic vegetables and fruit would be the primary food source. This value of preserving nature gave rise in the 70s and 80s to wellness lifestyles. American consumers in this generation are the most health-conscious among the general population.

Nonviolence
They coined the rallying cry, "Make love, not war!" The childhood of the baby boomers was spent in post-World War II peacetime. The Korean War did not affect them greatly, and it was generally viewed as a justifiable and necessary conflict. But Vietnam represented for this generation a betrayal of the peace promise. In the 70s and 80s the baby boomers used nonviolent means of resolving their conflicts. They are more amenable to bargaining, collaborating, and compromise than to confrontation to settle differences.

Creative Lifestyles
They lived in communes and created the sexual revolution. They explored alternative lifestyles ranging from rural com-

munities to traveling across the country in converted school buses painted in wild, psychedelic colors. The baby boomers are a much more mobile generation than others before them. In their work and living arrangements, they are much less willing to settle for traditional roles. They value freedom of movement and control of their own time more than the security and rewards of long-term employment.

Given these six values which drive baby boomers, how do they want to be treated as customers? Raines suggests at least five key issues will be critical in selling products and services to the baby boomer customer of the 1990s. "These factors can be generalized to most, but not all baby boomers," she says.

Relationship is More Important than Technique

These folks buy products and services from those whom they believe care about them as individuals. They value superior service more than any other group of consumers. They are willing to pay more for a product if they believe the person selling it to them is, or could become, a friend. If service is not personalized, and if the employee does not take the time to build a relationship with them, they are quickly turned off and will take their business elsewhere.

They Demand Undivided Attention

You have to remember that baby boomers grew up in post-World War II America where they were made the center of attention in their respective families. Their parents gave them everything they could, within their means. This was the generation that would land a man on the moon. Their self-centeredness carries over today in a demand to receive unique and undivided attention from sales persons.

Baby boomers have come to expect personal relationships with their bankers, doctors, insurance agents, waiters and waitresses, and lawyers. One of Texas's largest chain of department stores, Palais Royal, instituted a program of rewarding sales associates who called their customers by name. That's the kind of attention and reinforcement that the baby boomer customer demands.

They Resist External Motivation

These buyers want to make their own decisions, assisted by a friendly, personal sales representative. Remember, they have an innate value which tells them to distrust authority and big business. As a result, if they feel you are trying to use motivation techniques with them, they view the situation negatively. They don't like pushy salespeople, and they don't like to be hustled. They will not buy if they feel pressured.

They Choose Products That Reinforce Their Personal Value Systems

They care less about your product's benefits than they do about how it supports their current lifestyle. An example: a 35-year-old woman went shopping for a small television set. The salesman tried to convince her not to buy the small set, but to purchase a larger television that was on sale and would actually cost less than the smaller model. She remained adamant and practically had to beg the salesman to sell her the small-screen television set. The salesman failed to ask a central question, "Why do you need a smaller set?" If he had, he would have discovered that she wanted the set for a shelf in her bathroom where she could soak in a hot tub and watch her favorite television show.

Acknowledge Their Objections

Because they are driven by a fundamental need for harmony in relationships, it is a mistake to try to overcome the objections of this customer. They tend to be well-informed about the product or service they are interested in buying and may express their objections with a good deal of authority. Traditional sales techniques call for overcoming objections, but baby boomers will not buy if they sense they are going to have a battle about their concerns. You will get further with the baby boomer customers by acknowledging their objections and honoring them.

The Traditionalists

Members of the traditionalist generation were born before 1945. The younger members of this group are on the cusp with the end of the baby boom generation. They were born between 1941 and 1945 and share many of the same values as the older members of the baby boomer group.

This generation is now entering its late 40s and early 50s. They are at the peak of their earning potential and buying power. Older members of this generation comprise the current group of retirees.

Marketing researchers estimate there are approximately nine traditionalists for every ten baby boomers. They represent a much more affluent group up to age 65. Those in the 35 to 50 group will control 42 percent of household income by the year 2000. After 65 more of the traditionalists are retired and are on fixed income and social security. They have less discretionary purchasing power than the 50 to 65 crowd. Leisure time is higher among the traditionalist generation and there appears to be a move toward earlier retirement. Many companies in the late 80s downsized their employee workforces and offered early retirement to thousands of employees between the ages of 50 and 60.

Members of this generation are called traditionalists because they tend to cling to the traditional values held by Americans prior to, during, and shortly after WWII. Here is a useful comparison of the values driving the buying behaviors of traditionalists, compared with those of baby boomers:[7]

The Traditionalist	The Baby Boomer
1. Wants to be sold	1. Wants to be served
2. Buys American products	2. Buys imported products
3. Respects authority	3. Challenges authority
4. Honors tradition	4. Breaks from tradition
5. High brand loyalty	5. Influenced by fads
6. Vanilla, chocolate, strawberry	6. 31 flavors
7. Enjoys the "hard sell" game	7. Doesn't like to play games
8. Buys the best products	8. Buys the relationship first
9. Asks, "How is it best?"	9. Asks, "How is it different?"
10. Pays cash	10. Uses credit
11. One for all, all for one	11. Pursues self-interest
12. Buys what the market wants to sell	12. The market sells what they want to buy

Cultural Differences among Service Employees

We live in an increasingly diverse society. And this causes some problems. Consider the number of state ballot initiatives in recent years to declare English the official language.

Here's another example: most ocean cruise line companies employ culturally and racially mixed crew members to serve passengers. A typical cruise liner is like a floating United Nations. The officers and crew may include Norwegians, Italians, Indonesians, Chinese and Malaysians. Each of these ship employees bring certain cultural values, beliefs, attitudes and behaviors to the job. Obviously, not everyone has the same western perspective toward daily hygiene which we Americans tend to practice. As a result, sometimes passengers complain about employees with objectionable body odors, even though, from the foreign employee's perspective, it was probably the Americans who smelled bad!

Because of the baby bust generation there are fewer people available to perform frontline service jobs. Total births in the United States dropped from 72.5 million during the baby boom years to 56.6 million in the bust years. The effect of this shrinking entry-level labor pool is being felt today. You've no doubt seen the television commercial for McDonald's in which an older citizen, obviously retired, goes to work at a neighborhood McDonald's restaurant. McDonald's has launched a recruiting program called McMasters.

The impact on the customer out there is that more and more frontline service jobs are going to be filled by an increasingly diverse cultural mix of service employees because there simply aren't enough young people available to fill the needed vacancies. That is going to require a heightened sensitivity to other cultures on the part of American service employees. And it's going to require special training for the non-American who works in the American service economy.

Cultural Differences among Customers

The other major effect of our increasingly diverse economy is the number of non-English speaking customers. They, like culturally diverse service employees, bring with them their own set of inputs that create their frame of reference for doing business in the new economy. Have you taken the time to observe the cultural differences among your customer population?

An American company, Rent-A-Center, is a large furniture rental firm. With stores spaced throughout the Western United States, they serve an incredibly diverse group of customers. Some of their customers—migrant Hispanic workers—are in residence for a few months each year to pick agricultural crops. One person who speaks English well enough to communicate is chosen as the spokesman for the entire group. This single individual orders all the furniture for the entire group and collects the rental payments each week. "They are always on time with their payments and the furniture is always returned in excellent condition," says Frank Carney, company president. "Of course, we try to understand the nature of their work, and we place store managers who speak Spanish in those store locations whenever we can," he adds.

An important task, if you wish to make your business service-driven, is to examine the cultural diversity of your customer population. When service employees are ignorant of the values of other cultures who make up part of your customer base, the result can be a deterioration or loss of the moments of truth.

Cultural Drives among Americans

The products and services which you market and sell to your customers must be consistent with the values they hold. As Americans, we tend to be driven by certain cultural values that profoundly influence our behavior as customers.

The Drive to Take Action

We are a take-charge, time-driven society. Perhaps you've seen the bumper sticker proclaiming: "Lead, Follow, or Get the Hell Out of the Way!" The American consumer is constantly looking for ways to save, manage, borrow, and kill time. We have this drive to stay busy, and it causes some problems for us. You've probably heard about the Type A personality who is driven to constantly stay busy. You probably work with someone like this: a person who literally lives for his or her work. For this individual, work is indistinguishable from play. Often they look at other cultures that tend not to move as fast and frantically as they do, and perceive them as lazy, backward, passive, or slow. If this perception becomes an input into a service employee's frame of reference, you risk the possibility of offending customers and losing their loyalty.

The Drive to Acquire Material Goods

You have only to page through the daily paper, the national news magazines, or watch a few television commercials to realize how powerfully this value drives American consumer behavior. The old, "keeping up with the Joneses," is not enough anymore. We want to *be* the Joneses! We are a society which collects the signs and symbols of acquisition. We compare ourselves against others by matching our "collection" with theirs. Automobiles, houses, electronic goods, vacations, and clothing are only a few of the artifacts which consumers collect.

A recent newspaper story reported a new dress code for a large urban high school. The major change was in the prohibition of wearing designer clothing with conspicuous labels and, at the other end of the scale, wearing torn, faded, or otherwise inappropriate attire. Apparently young people at the high school judged one another by the designer labels. One young man refused to go to school because his family could not afford the "right" kind of shoes. The other prevailing group, the "have-nots", showed their defiance of the "haves" by counter-dressing in ragged, torn clothing.

The Drive to Work Hard and Play Hard

Americans are caught in a double bind. The generation preceding the baby boomers was driven by the Protestant work ethic. The generally accepted behavior was to join a company, remain a loyal employee, rise in the corporation, then enjoy your retirement years. The baby boom generation believes in working hard, too, but wants its reward much sooner. So while the consumer is one who is driven to work hard, the marketplace is full of products that are designed to relieve us of chores so we can spend more time in leisure activities! The sale of household cleaning products such as powder cleaners, detergents, mops, brooms, and so forth has been in a steady decline in recent years. Why? Because the number of two-earner homes has increased, and baby boomers do not want to spend time cleaning house when they can pursue a leisure activity. So they hire a cleaning service. There has been a boom in home cleaning services that shows no sign of abating.

The Drive to Buy Now and Pay Later

The natural extension of the "work hard and play hard" value is one that allows instant gratification. We live in a world of plastic money. The proliferation of credit cards and automated teller machines (ATMs) is staggering. It is currently estimated that we Americans are carrying around nearly *125 million* credit cards. We are constantly solicited by financial institutions pushing this gold card or that platinum one. The "buy now, pay later" value is not one found widely in the traditionalist generation, although the younger members of that generation tend to use credit more than do the older members. Traditionalists tend to save up money and pay cash for large purchases. Baby boomers check their line of credit and if they haven't "maxed out" are just as likely to make even relatively large purchases on credit.

The Drive to be Young, Good-looking, and Slim

One of the values which drives American consumers is an almost fanatical pursuit of that which makes us younger, more beautiful or handsome, and slimmer. When talk show host Oprah Winfrey announced that she had lost 67 pounds on a liquid diet, the manufacturer of the product was swamped by more than 1,000 calls *per hour.* An ever-increasing number of weight-loss clinics and centers spend hundreds of thousands of dollars proclaiming their success stories. And they earn even more by helping people who want to be thin.

There are increasing numbers of television commercials and newspaper advertisements for plastic surgeons willing to perform liposuction surgery, face lifts, breast augmentation or reduction surgery, nose jobs, chin jobs, eyelid jobs, ear jobs, and even derriere augmentation or reduction.

The cosmetics industry is booming. And not just for women. Cosmetics for men represent an increasing share of an already overcrowded market. The old barber shop is becoming an anachronism in the face of "total image" salons. We are a society that likes to feel good and look good, and we want others to know it.

There are hundreds of different values that drive customer behavior. What is important for our purposes here is that you understand the need to get into close touch with the values that drive *your* customers' behavior. Only when you know what factors are on your customers' report cards can you begin to build a business that puts the customer at the center and is truly customer-driven, which is critical to competitive success in the service revolution.

SERVICE PRODUCTS OF THE 1990s

The customers of the 1990s, especially the baby boomers and baby busters, are going to demand more services and higher quality of services than any previous generations. Driven by their respective value systems, they will insist upon a level of service that is a step beyond where most companies are today. In the new decade, service will be the primary product, and those companies that make service their driving force will be the ones who will gain the competitive edge. Here's just a sampling of some of the challenges facing American business.

The Travel Industry

The primary difference between the customer of the past and the customer of the 1990s is that the new decade customer will not want just a trip, but will want an *experience*. The increasing availability of expeditions which combine the vacation experience with a sense of adventure, and even danger, will become increasingly popular. Those from the baby boom generation will constitute a major source of customers for the travel industry in the years ahead. You can see this trend be-

ginning to happen already. The move is away from the tradi
tional two weeks vacation per year to shorter jaunts to
interesting places. The baby boom generation is more interested in long week-ends, taken several times a year.

At 10 A.M. one weekday morning, a major Denver radio
station offered the first 100 persons who showed up at the airport a free flight to Jamaica if they could be ready to leave at
2 P.M. that day. They were amazed at the number of people who
called in, and who could leave at a moment's notice. Many were
turned away.

You can also see the difference in how businesses handle
the vacation time of their employees. One of the latest trends
is to lump all the employee's sick time, vacation time, and personal leave time into one account, from which the employee
may draw days at his or her own discretion. If the employee
uses up all of the time account, any days taken because of illness are not paid.

In addition to travel agencies, transportation as a service
product will change during the new decade. With the tremendous increase in air travel, larger airports will be needed. Look
for increased technological means of moving great masses of
people and their luggage from one place to another. The huge
United Airlines terminal at Chicago's O'Hare Airport provides
a glimpse at what we can expect in airport design in the
future.

Cruise Lines

Ocean cruising as a vacation choice has gained tremendously
in popularity in recent years. Once viewed as the recreation of
the rich, cruises are now within the economic reach of a large
percentage of the population.

One of the major lessons learned by cruise lines in the
mid-80s is that the new cruise line customer is younger, more
health-oriented, and more destination-driven. The perceptions
of their passengers on the part of many cruise lines is still
grounded in a value system based upon conspicuous consumption. However, there appears to be a growing tendency on the
part of some ship companies to listen to what the customer

wants in a cruise experience and then to deliver it with extraordinary service.

We anticipate the product of the 1990s for cruise lines will emphasize much more of the shipboard experience with many more options available to passengers, such as healthy menus with low fat, low sodium and low cholesterol offerings; more exercise programs; more special interest cruises; and new and different ports of call.

There is already an increasing number of very small cruise ships that accommodate only a couple of hundred passengers and that can go into ports where the big ships cannot dock. These smaller luxury vessels give passengers a sense of visiting an out-of-the-way place where others have not gone before, thus meeting the expectation of an *adventure* and an *experience*.

Restaurant Customers

Clearly one of the most competitive and failure prone, the restaurant industry will have to examine its service product critically in the 1990s. Food and drink sales produced $147.6 billion income in 1987, the fourth highest in retail sales according to the Department of Commerce. Strangely enough, many restaurants, it seems, have still not caught on to the idea that superior service pays off. Restaurant customers continue to be among the most poorly treated of all consumer groups and, more amazingly, they keep coming back for more! It's no secret that restaurant workers are among the lowest paid of salaried workers, and they depend heavily on tips they receive to supplement their income. It is puzzling why so many of them engage in surly, uncaring behaviors. The next time you dine out, see if your waiter or waitress suddenly gets friendlier when it's about the time to present your check.

Restaurant customers today demand a wider choice of healthier foods prepared the way they want. Many restaurants have begun to include menu items cooked with low fat, sodium, and cholesterol, in response to the customer's requirements. We believe this trend will continue into the next decade with increased popularity. New restaurants are opening daily and just as many fail. The restaurant of the 1990s will offer a service product that distinguishes it from the competition and will match the uniqueness of its product with a superior level of service. To do less will be to risk failure.

Hotel Customers

Amenities packages sell $60 million a year to the hotel industry. Hilton Hotels spends $225,000 on an average night to provide *bathroom* amenities to its guests. *Frequent Flyer* magazine recently carried a piece that reported that amenities such as soaps, shampoos, mouthwashes, shower caps, sewing kits, shoehorns, and shoe mitts are becoming increasingly important with business travelers, the hotel industry's bread and butter trade. Hilton spent two years coming up with the right package of amenities after an analysis of consumer trends showed their competition was outspending them and that consumer tastes were changing.

Hotel customers are picky about the quality of the amenities provided. Dennis Wagner, vice president of operations for Marriott, said, "We do several surveys a year to find out what people want. We also ask how they like what we have, how often they use it, and, to keep ahead, we ask what they might want in the future."[8]

The hotel industry does a better job than most others of staying in touch with its customers. At least, the successful ones do. Some of them, however, mistake the level of amenities for the quality of service; but if the basics aren't done well (e.g., dirty room, unfriendly staff, etc.) the amenities don't help. Inevitably, hotels will have to get inside the heads of their guests, as Marriott has done, to continue to meet current expectations, and to anticipate future trends among their customers.

The Portman Hotel in San Francisco prides itself on its extraordinary service. Offering 24 hour *gourmet* room service, no predetermined check-out time, and rooms and suites richly appointed in brass, marble, rosewood, and mahogany, the Portman is clearly not targeting the family vacation customer. Whenever a person enters a room or suite, the personal valet leaves a broom bristle at the door. When it has been disturbed, the valet knows the customer has left and tidies up the room, replaces towels, and in general brings things back to a "just walked-in" appearance. On differing scales, that's the level of service to which successful hotels will ascribe in the 1990s.

Changing Role of Health Care Customers

Hospitals, clinics, health maintenance organizations, and physicians in private practice have felt the impact of increasing competition, increasing governmental regulation, insurance costs, and a much more demanding health care customer.

In years past, the patient was just that—*patient*. That meant doing what your doctor told you to do, going where your doctor told you to go, waiting without complaint, and showing respect for anyone who wore a medical uniform or carried a stethoscope. The times have changed. Today's health care customers are much more literate in medical matters. They are exposed to a barrage of medical information, both on television and in print.

Research conducted at Santa Monica Hospital in Santa Monica, California revealed that customers valued trust and credibility more than any other single variable of health care. In other words, they wanted to know they could rely on their hospital to give them accurate and timely information concerning their progress and medical care.

When physicians who admitted patients to the hospital were surveyed, Santa Monica Hospital discovered something interesting. Nearly 55 percent of patients who had to be hospitalized expressed to their physicians a definite preference for a specific hospital. This represented a significant change from the "doctor knows best" mindset. It also represented a virtually untapped source of medical customers—physicians.

Today's health care consumer is more critical, more demanding, better educated, and, in some cases, willing to pay a higher cost for medical care. Some hospitals provide rooms that rival the best hotels, offering gourmet food and even wine service. Providing a suite for the new parents-to-be with built-in video transmission from the delivery room is becoming more and more common. Of course, these upscale facilities cost more. But there seem to be customers who are willing to pay for the extra amenities and service.

SERVICE CONTEXTS OF THE 1990S

In Chapter 2 we introduced the service context, the setting in which the customer encounters your business and experiences the moments of truth that add up to his or her estimation of the quality of service in your business. Here are some service contexts that will be affected by a stronger consumer demand for quality service in the 1990s.

Telephone Contact With Customers

Organizations constantly look for ways to use time more efficiently. In the late 80s there was an explosion of interest in automated, computer-driven telephone systems. What all of these systems have in common is that they free the employee to do other things. Along with efficiency has come depersonalization. Originally intended to be used when the employee was away from his or her desk and to send messages internally, many automated telephone systems have become full-time telephone answering machines. Employees and managers simply don't answer the telephone personally anymore. The result is that you get to talk to a computer, and the game of telephone tag has become one that is microchip controlled.

One large company recently installed an automated system. When you call this company you no longer talk to a human being. Instead, you interact with the computer, leaving messages in the phone mail system. You call. You enter the phone mail system. You leave the recorded message. Five minutes later, your party calls back to discuss the message you left on the phone mail. So what could have been done with one call now takes two.

The biggest disadvantage of these wonderfully efficient systems, from a service standpoint, is that they have effectively removed human interaction from the moment of truth. While the need to manage telephone calls has given rise to the automated systems, we can't help but wonder if there isn't a detrimental effect upon the overall quality of service. The counterargument is that the automated systems have eliminated customers being placed on hold for long periods of time, unanswered telephones, and busy signals. We don't disagree. Our concern is that when humans interact with machines, you lose the opportunity to influence the customer in a personal way.

Television Shopping

If you have cable television you have seen the merchandise shopping programs. These programs are almost like game shows where contestants vie for Door 1, Door 2, or Door 3. With pseudoauction atmosphere, they are hosted by vivacious men and women who pitch their products through the television medium much as the traveling salesman sold household goods from the back of a horse-drawn wagon.

These shopping programs—many of them portray themselves as clubs—have proliferated in recent years. A number of them have started and failed to survive in an extremely competitive video market. One that has outperformed and outdistanced all the others is the Home Shopping Club (HSC). With sales of more than $1 billion per year, HSC estimates it can sell up to $10 billion in merchandise per year through television.

"Sixty Minutes" recently profiled the HSC operation. In a huge television studio sit dozens of telephone operators, "waiting to take your call." And the system works beautifully. One of the corporate officers who was interviewed stated that their success was due to "superior customer service." We found his comments to be striking. He explained that customers want a return to the good old days when they were treated as individuals, not as a number.

Scenes from the program showed operators speaking to customers who were placing orders by telephone for merchandise offered for sale. The operators were personable, polite, friendly, smiling at their invisible customers, and calling them by name. The show also creates a family effect. Frequently customers call in during the program to tell how much they liked a product they purchased. They get to be on the air with the show's host, who talks to them as though they are old friends.

The contrast between the telephone operations of cable television merchandising programs like Home Shopping Club and the automated telephone systems is worth noting. Both are efficient systems. Both allow the customer to make instant contact with the business. Yet, one company capitalizes on the system by personalizing its service, and the other removes personalization.

The Fax Phenomenon

Facsimile transmitting devices, popularly known as "fax machines", have become *de rigueur* for the busy executive, manager, and entrepreneur. Geoffrey Richards, an Australian management consultant, reports that the latest development in his country is that sales representatives carry portable fax machines with them, along with car telephones, so they can stay in contact with customers and the home office while traveling Australia's vast reaches.

The conventional wisdom predicts that fax machines will become as common in the 1990s as pocket calculators. Rapidly dropping in price as new telecommunication technologies advance, fax machines are among the fastest growing segments of the communications industry. Documents from virtually anywhere in the world can be on your desk in a matter of seconds. The added cost is well worth the time saved.

But how will the explosive proliferation of fax machines affect the customer of the 1990s? If the conventional wisdom holds true, and if fax machines begin to find their way into homes as well as into businesses, we can expect a concurrent flood of fax-based merchandising schemes. It's happening already. A new problem has developed: *fax junk*. Enterprising businesses simply send promotional material to your fax number. Not only does it cost in terms of tying up telephone circuits, but to add insult to injury, it is your paper being used to print someone else's marketing information!

Customers and ATMs

The first automatic teller machine (ATM) was installed in Valdosta, Georgia in 1970. Since then, the technology behind these money machines has evolved significantly. You can get money from your account in literally thousands of locations throughout the world. The ATM has, without a doubt, contributed to the productivity of live tellers by freeing them of many time-consuming, routine banking transactions. And they have created a unique service context for the 1990s. Any bank customer can now be within a few seconds and a plastic card of his or her bank account, anywhere in the world. Surprisingly little research has been done in recent years to determine the banking customer's response to ATMs.

What we do know is that ATMs would not have been possible unless customers were willing to forego personal contact with tellers for the convenience of automation. Of course, maybe the quality of their contacts wasn't very good in the first place. And that leads us back to our earlier point about computer-driven telephone systems. You can't deny their efficiency and convenience. Yet ATMs, like the phone mail systems, eliminate human contact from the service context.

The result is that when customers do actually enter the bank the quality of service is more important than ever before. Financial analyst Jeremy Main says, "Perhaps the most competitive service a bank can offer is what bankers call a relationship, which means the customer gets to deal with a real human being, preferably one who is knowledgeable and courteous and who will get to know his name and history."[9]

Using a new tactic, begun in 1989, Bank of America and Wells Fargo began to charge their ATM customers 30 cents to $1.25 for each transaction. When questioned by reporters as to the public's response to these charges, one bank officer quipped, "They have to go along with it." So much for being customer-focused.

We believe that ATMs will continue to evolve technologically and, in spite of being charged for their transactions, customers will continue to use them. We also believe that banking institutions will have to find innovative ways to offset the negative impact of decreasing numbers of human contacts between their customers and their institutions. Fewer human moments of truth mean that each individual moment of truth becomes more critical.

Service Quality as Perceived by Customers

As we noted earlier, organizations often perceive the quality of service quite differently than do their customers. Physicians often equate the technical quality of care with the quality of service. Utility companies believe their reliability in producing electricity and their ability to restore power during outages equals superior service. Restaurants often operate on the premise that if the food is prepared well and tastes good, then they have a right to the customer's loyalty.

But the quality of service as perceived by customers in the 1990s will be markedly different from the perceptions of years past. A juxtaposition of technology and the efficient systems it creates may clash with the need for human contact with customers. Thus, in the decade ahead, the customer's perception of service may be focused more on the recovery record of business when technical systems fail. Customers like convenience and timesaving devices. But they also want a live, warm, breathing human being close by when the automated system doesn't do what it is supposed to do.

Also, the differing values systems that will drive the customer of the 1990s will affect the perception of service. There are some early signs that young people in the late 80s are resurrecting clothing styles and symbols from the 60s. These youngsters, mostly in their preteen years, may carry a completely different value system into the service context of the 1990s. We will have to watch the trend and see.

The Disneyland Context

Disneyland is a remarkable example of a total service context. In few other places have the social, physical, psychological, and interpersonal elements been so effectively interwoven to create a superior service context. Employees are not "employees," and they don't do "jobs" at "the company." Each person hired is a "character" who "plays a role" in "the show." Each person has his or her own special "costume" that is consistent with one of the park's major themes. So you won't see someone wearing a western outfit in Tomorrowland, even if he or she is playing the role of streetsweeper.

Young people hired as employees by Disneyland are often interviewed in groups of three. The interviewer focuses as much on how the candidate relates to and interacts with the other two candidates, as to the candidate's answers to interview questions. The natural smile and a genuinely sparkling personality are important job related factors.

The result of all this is that Disneyland creates a total service context in which the customer is put first at all times. If you roamed throughout the park and asked employees what the product of Disneyland is, the common refrain would be, "We create happiness!" The single-minded focus on making a visit to Disneyland *an experience* is what distinguishes Walt Disney's legacy from other amusement parks throughout the country.

The Westin Kauai Service Context

The flagship of the new super hotels, the Westin Kauai, located in Lihue on the island of Kauai, Hawaii, creates a special service context. With a multimillion dollar display of fine Oriental art and stunning architecture, the hotel has created a fantasy resort experience.

The level of service by all employees is extraordinarily high. After all, guests at this new hotel may be paying up to several hundred dollars per night for the luxury treatment. The groundskeeping staff is carefully uniformed in quasimilitary khaki safari suits, complete with pith helmets. They go about their tasks unobtrusively. All service personnel wear uniforms that are compatible with their work. And they are called *performers*, not *employees*.

The overall effect is the creation of a service context in which everything works, and things happen when they are supposed to. You get the impression that the hotel has a system of procedures with one purpose in mind: to make the paying guest as comfortable as possible.

The Fast Friends Context

Have you noticed the difference between the way a new customer at a place of business is treated when compared to a regular? Why is it that the new customer receives a rather formal, cold greeting, and the regular customer is met like an old friend? Why do regulars get served first? Why does the atmosphere change when the new customer arrives?

The answers to these questions lie in the service context created when the regular customer comes in. A relationship with the firm has been established. The service personnel have come to know this customer's foibles. What has happened is that the service employee has come to really know the customer. The customer's likes and dislikes have been learned over a period of time.

We suggest that new customers should be treated the same as regulars. That requires creating what we call the "fast friends" context. It means that service employees should meet and greet new customers with the same enthusiasm and interpersonal style they use to welcome their regular customers. After all, the regulars were new customers themselves at one time. It also will require you to find out what is on your customers' report cards so that you'll know how to treat them as fast friends.

The Customer as Enemy Context

It's hard to believe that any business would see its customers as enemies. The fact is, many do—many unconsciously, some consciously. Often the overworked, stressed, and exhausted doctor or nurse will come to view the next patient with resentment. Knowing that person represents perhaps another three hours in surgery or yet another series of complaints to be dealt with, the medical professional, without malice aforethought, begins to view the customer as an enemy.

When that happens, you can imagine the service context that is created at the moment when doctor or nurse and patient come to the moment of truth. Exhausted bodies and burned-out psyches don't lend themselves to creating a customer-focused service context.

If you are in a business where there is a high level of contact with angry customers, you are susceptible to the customer as enemy phenomenon. Consider the job of the utility company's customer service representatives. They sit at computer terminals all day long, fielding call after call from customers, many of them irate. It is easy to see how the customer can come to be resented by the person providing the service.

Businesses will have to look for ways to help employees "stay up" in stressful occupations. And service employees will need to look within to discover their own stress management zones so they know when they are approaching the customer as enemy point of tolerance.

WHAT BUGS CUSTOMERS

The customer's perception of the quality of service lies in the details. One can speculate that it would probably be worse to be nibbled to death by ants than stomped to death by an elephant. The metaphor applies to the delivery of service. Customers can be a very understanding lot when they know you're making a real effort to make things right. That's the elephant. You can avoid the big ones because they are usually pretty obvious and hard to hide. But when you let the little things go, that's when the ants start their march, and that's when customers get bugged.

Seven Sins of Service

In *At America's Service,* Karl identified seven common sins of service. These sins happen repeatedly and are among the most common blunders that bug customers. There are really only a few things that really anger and aggravate customers. Here they are.

Treating Customers with Apathy

In its worst form, apathy happens when the service employee says to the customer, "Look me in the eye and try to imagine how little I care." Research on what burns-out employees leads us to believe that apathy is an early sign of an employee who has retired on-the-job. When service employees stop caring about their work, their customers, and themselves, it's time to make a change, either personal or professional.

Brushing Customers Off

This sin of service happens when the employee tries to get rid of the customer. Usually it's triggered by the employee's desire to do something else. The thought process of a person committing the brush-off sin is, "If it weren't for all these customers, I could get some work done around here!" The idea is to get rid of the customer as quickly as possible.

Here's a true incident to illustrate the point: a customer approached a car rental counter in the Oakland, California airport. Two agents were stationed behind the counter. One of them was busy with someone else, so the customer approached the second agent, who was rubber-stamping a big stack of forms. The customer said, "Excuse me, my name is Jones and I have a reserved car." Without missing a beat with the rubber stamp, and without looking up, the agent said, "You'll have to see my partner. It's almost five o'clock and I'm trying to get out of here." That's the brush-off.

Being Cold toward Customers

You've experienced it, haven't you? The overly formal and un-smiling waiter? The officious hotel clerk with the surgically implanted mask that shows no emotion? The service context quickly becomes cold: chilly reception, cold shoulder, icy stare, and the cold heart are phrases that come to mind to describe this scene.

The most tragic setting for this service sin is the very place where people should never experience it: medical care facilities. Some medical personnel seem to have received emotional bypass operations. The coldness with which some patients are treated is amazing. There seems to be a cause and effect connection between becoming burned-out and treating others with coldness. The flame of human compassion just isn't there any more, and it's the customer who suffers the consequences.

Treating Customers with Condescension
Talking down to customers, using jargon they can't understand, shouting at elderly persons and those who don't speak English very well, and brushing children aside are just a few of the ways that condescension is practiced. When customers are patronized and belittled, they remember it. And they take their business someplace else.

Working Like a Robot
Has it ever occurred to you that a sizable portion of the population is running around unconscious? Ted Willey, a Denver-based management consultant who conducts workshops in personal responsibility, calls this "going unk." When a person becomes so routinized that he or she does everything the same way, day after day, the service sin of robotism can creep into daily behavior toward customers.

A case in point: a business traveler boarded his airplane in Chicago, and the first sight he encountered was an unsmiling flight attendant. "Why don't you smile?" he asked, hoping to cheer her up. "I'll tell you what," the attendant said. "You smile first, then I will." So the man smiled. "Good!" was the reply, "Now just hold it that way for the next 12 hours and see how you like it!" And with that the attendant turned away. Here, robotism was exceeded only by the customer as enemy perception.

Getting Hung Up on the Rule Book
It happens all the time. When an organization's rules and regulations are created more for its convenience than for the convenience of the customer, you increase the chance that somebody is going to commit the rule book service sin. It works like this: a man entered the lobby of a hospital's emergency room and began pushing a wheelchair out to his car to help his wife, who couldn't walk. He was stopped by a nurse who told him he couldn't use the wheelchair and would have to go into the hospital's basement, leave his driver's license, and then he

could check out a wheelchair. When he inquired as to why, since his wife was sitting in the car barely 20 feet away, he should have to trudge over to the hospital, over a half block distant, he was told, "Those are just our rules." This incident happened beneath a big banner the hospital had put up proclaiming, "We're here for you!"

If you want to make your organization service-focused, you will have to empower your people to make common sense common practice. Sometimes, it seems there's not much common sense being practiced out there.

Giving Customers the Runaround

Pushing the customer around the organization's pillars and posts is a variation of the brush-off sin of service discussed earlier. The runaround is a way to get rid of the customer so the employee can do something else. Does this sound familiar? "I'd like to help you, but that's not this department. You need to go down the hall, take a left and a right and a left and you'll find someone to help you . . . oh, sir? . . . Have a nice day!" The next time you make a phone call to a business, count the number of times you are handed off before you find someone who can help you with your problem. That's the runaround quotient.

We live in an increasingly litigious society. Consumers of the 1990s are going to be more militant. They're mad as hell, and they're not going to take it anymore. When the customer of the 1990s becomes the victim of a service sin, he or she is much more likely to seek redress. Of course, most of your customers' responses won't involve lawsuits. Most of them will just stop doing business with you. If you want to keep a competitive edge, sooner or later you'll have to deal with those managers and employees who commit the sins of service.

WHO WILL BE THE SERVICE WINNERS OF THE 1990s?

We believe the service winners in the 1990s will be those companies who take a wholly different approach to the subject of customer service. The service winners will be businesses who make the customer the focal point of everything they do. They will, literally, become *customer-driven*. That means that they will gain an intimate knowledge of their customers to a degree previously unheard of. *Newsweek* recently interviewed John Lee, CEO of Chas. A. Stevens, an upscale seller of women's clothing for a story on the changing woman customer. After a disastrous attempt to introduce a high-priced miniskirted line of fashions into the market, Lee said he learned his lesson. He vowed to track a typical customer so well that "I'm going to know what she eats for breakfast."[10]

That's the kind of thinking that's going to separate the service winners from the service losers. Those companies that insist on following the old, "We know what's best for our customers" paradigm will make a fatal mistake in the service contexts of the 1990s. Only those companies that make a fetish of knowing the minds of their customers will thrive in the decade ahead.

NOTES

1. "Management for the 1990s," *Newsweek*, April 25, 1988, p. 47.
2. Ron Zemke, "Training in the '90s," *Training*, January 1987, p. 43.
3. Robert B. Settle and Pamela L. Alreck, *Why They Buy: American Consumers Inside and Out* (New York: John Wiley & Sons, 1986), p. 250.
4. Lawrence Graham and Lawrence Hamdan, *Youth Trends: Capturing the $200 Billion Youth Market* (New York: St. Martin's Press, 1987), p. 11.
5. Landon Y. Jones, *Great Expectations: America and the Baby Boom Generation* (New York: Ballantine Books, 1981), p. 256.
6. Claire Raines, *The Big Chill Generation at Work*™, book manuscript in progress, 1988.
7. Ibid.
8. "Room at the Top," *Frequent Flyer*, May 1987, p. 43.
9. Jeremy Main, "How Banks Lure the Rich," *Fortune*, November 1, 1982, p. 62.
10. Patricia King, "The High Price of Unhappy Customers," *Newsweek*, December 5, 1988, p. 64.

CHAPTER 4

THE CUSTOMER REPORT CARD: BLUEPRINT FOR EXCELLENCE

You want your business to stand out from your competition. You want your current customers to stay with you for the long-term and you want to attract and keep new customers. To create a lasting service advantage will require up-to-date and accurate information about every aspect of your customers.

It's dangerous, from a service standpoint, to assume that you know your customers well. Businesses that have active marketing, public relations, or research departments often believe they know everything they need to about their customers. Some do. But a surprising number of them don't. Worse, some businesses assume that "no news is good news" and if customers aren't complaining they must be satisfied. That's a risky assumption. You must, on a regular basis, take the pulse of your customers, because their expectations constantly change. Not only that, economic conditions and the whims of the marketplace are variable.

And there's another fact to consider: customers are different and have different needs, even within fairly close geographical confines. A company in a college or university city will likely have a greater proportion of customers who attend college or who have earned college degrees. The same company could have a branch office in another part of the city where industry and factory workers make up the general population. Same company, same products, but different locations and different customer bases.

But suppose you're not a big company. You don't have a marketing or public relations department. Maybe you're a small business owner with only a few dozen employees. Or, perhaps you're a sole proprietor who does just about everything yourself. You still face the same challenge as bigger businesses, with all their support functions. You, like they, must have a blueprint for excellence; a systematic method for assessing your customer's inputs: attitudes, values, beliefs, wants, feelings, and expectations. That blueprint is the customer report card.

WHAT IS A CUSTOMER REPORT CARD?

A customer report card is a physical, tangible, management tool. It functions very much the same way as the report card a young person brings home from school. The school report card contains a list of subjects and a grade that indicates the quality of performance in each course. In other words, it provides real data and a structured way of looking at the student's work over a period of time.

The customer report card provides data, from the customer's perspective, on your service performance. What is different is that instead of a list of subjects, as the school student has, your report card contains four kinds of information:

1. The key service quality attributes.
2. The relative desirability and importance of each attribute to your customer.
3. Your company's scores on these attributes.
4. The attributes and scores of your competition, if applicable.

The Key Service Quality Attributes

When we use the phrase, "service quality attribute" for the first time, a lot of people get a blank look, that is, a TEGO reaction (the eyes glaze over). The service quality attribute is to the customer report card as the subject of mathematics is to your youngster's report card from school. It is a tangible, measurable aspect of your business, as perceived by your customers.

These "service subjects" or attributes are created during the many moments of truth customers experience whenever they encounter any part of your business. Every customer carries around in his or her head a semiconscious grading system that is triggered whenever a moment of truth occurs.

Example: Think about your favorite restaurant; it's a place you enjoy going to for that special occasion dinner, such as an anniversary or birthday celebration. Now think of the attributes you carry with you, that is, your expectations about this special place. They probably include some of the following:

LesSpecial French Restaurant

1. You can reserve a table.
2. Parking or valet parking is available.
3. There is a coat check room.
4. All the employees will be friendly and courteous.
5. A maitre d' will greet you and show you to your table.
6. You will have a leisurely dinner without being rushed.
7. The food will be prepared properly, presented attractively, and taste good.
8. The entire restaurant will be clean, with no visible trash containers.
9. You can pay by credit card.
10. The dinner will be expensive.

These are the service quality attributes by which you will grade *LesSpecial* during your dining experience. There may be others you can think of, too.

By comparison, think of the service quality attributes you carry with you when you go to a fast food restaurant such as McDonald's, Burger King, or Wendy's:

Fast Food Restaurants

1. There will be ample parking and easy street access.
2. Lines will not be too long and will move quickly.
3. Food signs will clearly list products and prices.

4. All the employees will be friendly and courteous.
5. You will be able to get in and eat quickly.
6. The entire restaurant will be clean. Trash containers will be available.
7. The food will be prepared properly, presented attractively, and taste good.
8. You will pay with cash.
9. The meal will be inexpensive.

Notice which attributes hold true in both the elegant restaurant and the fast food restaurant. Some, such as parking, cleanliness, friendliness and courtesy, and food quality are the same for both places. The others are specific to the type of restaurant and, especially, to your expectations as the customer. You might, for instance, not notice a soda straw on the floor of a fast food restaurant, but it will stand out much more if you see it on the floor of your fancy restaurant. And you don't expect a maitre d' to seat you or to eat from fine china at McDonald's.

While there may be many attributes, and all of them have some degree of importance, you'll probably find there are only a relative few that you will label as *key service quality attributes*. In the examples above, you'd probably select cleanliness and food quality as key service attributes. Of course, there may be others as well, depending on your preferences as a customer.

The Relative Desirability and Importance of the Attributes

As we've noted, the very appearance of a service attribute on your customer's report card is an indication that it has some importance. But how much? What you want to know is how desirable or how important a particular attribute may be. Customers don't necessarily attach the same weight to all attributes. What you think is critical to the customer may be only of passing interest in the customer's view. On the other hand, your customer may be carrying around an attribute that he or she expects of your business that has never occurred to you. In the next and subsequent chapters we will explain in detail how to discover these attributes.

Your Company's Scores on the Service Attributes

Just as junior receives a grade for each course on his report card, so is the quality of your service rated by the customer. Once you've discovered the attributes that are important to your customers, and have attached a valence, or weight of importance to each of them, you still need to know what kinds of grades you're getting.

This is where a lot of businesses make a mistake. They believe they must be doing a good job on service because they hear few, if any complaints. Don't make the mistake of this assumption. As we'll see later, silence is not necessarily agreement.

You have to check your customer report card fairly frequently. Attributes that were important to your customer in the first half of the year may have changed. There may be new ones to be concerned about and some of the old ones may have dropped off the list.

THE CUSTOMER REPORT CARD IS CRUCIAL TO BUSINESS SUCCESS

We're going to presume that you're interested in taking your particular company or business operation to a service-driven level. Before you can begin to design tactics and strategies to do that, you have to know what is important to your customers. As we'll see a bit further on, it is not enough to just know who your customers are; you have to find out what makes them buy and what is important in terms of the quality of service.

The report card is crucial to your business success because it is your direct contact with the frames of reference of your customers. It just doesn't make sense to forge ahead with training programs about guest relations and improved service if you don't have a clear picture of what's on people's minds. The customer report card is the starting point for improved service. It can be used as the regular measurement tool any time you want to check up on the quality of service in your business. An often overlooked benefit of maintaining an accurate and up-to-date customer report card is that it can serve as a very powerful means of helping your service employees understand what they need to do to satisfy customers.

DISCOVERING YOUR CUSTOMER REPORT CARD

We've devoted an entire chapter to this subject further on; however, let's introduce briefly the major ways you can find out what is on your customers' respective report cards. We'll have a lot more to say about these methods and how to use them in the chapters that follow. There are three questions to consider:

1. Who are your customers?
2. What service attributes are most important to them?
3. How are you doing in meeting their service requirements?

Who Are Your Customers?

Before you can discover the customer report card you have to be sure you know who your customers are. The obvious category are those who do business with you, buying your product or service. These are *first level customers*. A phrase from your old high school Latin classes is useful here: *sine qua non*. Loosely translated, it means, "without which, nothing." A good way to identify your first level customers is to ask the question, "Whom do we depend upon in order to conduct our business?" You have to identify those customers about whom you could truly say, "without which, we are nothing." For example, in a hospital, the first level customer is probably the patient. But where does the hospital get its patients? From the physicians who admit them.

That leads to the next category: those customers with whom you may have a mutual interdependence. We call these *second level customers.* While it's true that a hospital's first level customer is the patient, there would be no patients if there were no physicians to admit them to the hospital. The physicians, in turn, are mutually dependent upon the hospital to provide the facilities, operating rooms and other support needed to provide medical and surgical treatment of patients.

But the physician cannot provide care without the help and support of a lot of other people. So there is another category called *third level customers.* These are often your own employees or persons outside the company that make it possible for you to conduct your business. Continuing our hospital example, the physician is dependent upon the nurse and myriad specialists and technicians to provide medical care. Ambulance companies, volunteers, third party insurance payers, linen supply companies, manufacturers of medical instruments, and vendors of the many different products needed to run a hospital are all part of the third level customer category.

There's one more category: *fourth level customers.* They may not have direct interaction with your business, but they're important to your success. In a medical setting this category includes florists, chaplains, family members of patients, local media, and government officials, among others.

By separating your customers into first, second, third, and fourth level categories, you can determine which customer report cards you need to focus upon first in order to gain a service advantage. You will also have a framework for making business decisions about your service improvements.

What Do Customers Want?

This is where you try to discover your customers' important service attributes. The simplest, most direct route to these attributes is to ask your customers directly. Many businesses conduct numerous surveys of their customers. Surveys can be very useful sources of information. But our concern is that most companies with whom we've worked seem to ask only those questions on surveys that *they* want to know the answers to. It seldom occurs to them to first find out what is important to the customer, *then* create a survey or questionnaire that reflects the items customers say they are interested in.

The most common method for discovering what is important to customers is the focus group. A focus group is a small group of 8 to 12 volunteers selected from your customer population. Using a special interviewing process, these folks reveal the service quality attributes which they hold important when they come to do business with you. Focus groups don't tell you what all customers think, but they do give you an idea of what is important to a sampling of your customers. Surveys and questionnaires can then be used to verify the focus group information with a larger customer population. We'll say much more about this later on when we take you step-by-step through the process of survey methods.

How Are You Doing, in Meeting Their Service Requirements?

When you answer this third question, you're going after your service grade point average. Once you've determined who your customers are, internally and externally, you can then use the focus group method to uncover key service quality attributes. By surveying a representative sample of your customers, you can verify the existence and importance of these key service quality attributes.

Part of the surveying process is to ask your customers to score your business on the level of performance for each of the service factors you wish to assess. When these data are obtained, you will have the basis for determining how well you are meeting your customers' expectations.

You still need to know how to do all of this, and the following chapters will take you through the process step-by-step.

A SAMPLE CUSTOMER REPORT CARD

The figure below shows a customer report card from a large health maintenance organization (HMO) in Nevada. The service attributes and scores were discovered through a combina-

FIGURE 4–1
HMO Customer Report Card

HMO CUSTOMER REPORT CARD		
Service Attribute	*Priority*	*Score*
1. Location of the clinic	Medium	B
2. Appointment availability	High	C
3. Having a personal physician	Medium	C
4. Waiting times	Low	C
5. Courteous employees	High	B
6. Telephone access	High	D
7. Understanding the bill	Medium	C
8. Cost of service	High	B
9. Quality of care	High	A

tion of focus group interviews and surveys of the HMO's members.

The Need to Segment Some Report Cards

The report card in Figure 4–1 is a general summary of service attributes which research revealed to be of importance to the HMO's customers. It is sometimes necessary to segment some report cards by category, especially if a large number of attributes emerge as important.

For example, service attribute number four, "Waiting times", could be segmented by measuring various parts of the HMO's operations. Service priorities and scores could be developed for waiting time in the reception rooms; waiting time in laboratory, X ray, or pharmacy; waiting in the physician's examining room; or waiting time in the cafeteria.

It becomes apparent that while waiting time to see a physician might have high priority with the customer, waiting times in the cafeteria might have low priority. At the same time, the service grade might be C for the doctor and A for the cafeteria. It is important to establish the importance of a service attribute to customers and not rely entirely on the score given.

Report Card for Employees

It is just as important to examine the attributes on your employees' report cards as it is to measure external customer perceptions. These attributes, commonly called "quality of work life" (QWL), come from the employees' perceived quality of all the aspects of their relationship with the organization. After all, the quality of work life, as perceived by the employees, has a direct and powerful influence on how they treat one another and your paying customers.

The external customer grades you on the quality of your service. The employee grades you on the QWL factors. These factors are part of the important inputs that help create your service employees' frames of reference, and that they bring to the moment of truth.

Much research has been done to identify the generic QWL factors held important by most employees. It's important to remember that these elements must be defined from the employees perspective, not that of management. If the employee believes the factor is part of the quality of his or her work life, then it is, whether management agrees or not. Some of the more frequently mentioned (not in order of importance) are:

1. *A job worth doing;* one that makes a worthwhile contribution to the objectives of the organization and that calls upon a reasonable share of the employee's skills, knowledge, and capabilities.
2. *Adequate working conditions;* a safe and reasonably humane set of physical and psychological conditions immediately surrounding the performance of the job.
3. *Adequate pay and benefits* in return for competent work.
4. *Job security;* knowing that one has a reasonable assurance of a job tomorrow if one is willing to work.
5. *Competent supervision;* positive, supportive, and affirmative treatment by one's boss and by higher levels of management.
6. *Feedback on the results of one's work;* recognition and

appreciation of one's contribution to the objectives of the organization.

7. *Opportunities for growth and development* in work skills and in responsibilities; progressively more challenging work which develops or activates progressively larger skills.

8. *A fair chance to get ahead on merit;* access to training, visibility to upper management, and competitive opportunities to win promotion to higher levels.

9. *A positive social climate;* a work setting that is stable, psychologically reinforcing, and humane in terms of values and interpersonal processes.

10. *Justice and fair play;* a sense that those in charge value and emphasize fairness and equitable treatment of all employees, regardless of social or ethnic concerns.[1]

While these are generic QWL factors and most of them probably apply to your business, it is important that you determine those that are specific to your own organization. These QWL factors make up the employee report card. In a service-driven business, everyone treats everyone else as a customer. In that context, it is vitally important to stay on top of what is making your employees tick and what is important to them. You can discover these QWL attributes with the same methods used to find out about your external customer report card. Put simply, in two words: *ask them.* You could present a list of these QWL factors to your employees and ask them to rate your business on a one to five scale. The results might be surprising.

Do Your Homework

As we noted at the beginning of this book, few businesses have much more than a basic understanding of their customers' needs, wants, values, attitudes, and beliefs. To gain the service advantage you'll need to gather the most complete and accurate information you can from all your customers.

Ignorance may be bliss, but in a competitive business environment it would be dangerous and foolish to subscribe to such a philosophy when it comes to your customers.

NOTES

1. Karl Albrecht, *Organization Development: A total systems approach to positive change in any business organization,* (Englewood Cliffs, NJ: Prentice-Hall, 1983), p. 77.

CHAPTER 5

CUSTOMER PERCEPTION RESEARCH: PUTTING ON YOUR CUSTOMERS' GLASSES

Maybe you remember going to a 3-D movie when you were a youngster, where you were given a pair of special glasses to wear while watching the movie. When you put them on, the movie's action seemed to jump off the screen and into your lap. But if you took them off, the screen was nothing but a flat, blurred, mass. Viewing your business through the glasses your customers wear is much like going to a 3-D movie. You need their special lenses if you want to see what they see, the way that they see it.

Seeing things as the customer does is important for another reason. When you are able to see your business the way your customers see it, you have stepped into that person's frame of reference. And when you get into another person's frame of reference, you get into their view of reality. That old saw, "the customer is always right," is only true up to a point. Yes, the customer is always right from his or her perspective. And you or your service employee are always right, from your own perspective. But it's really a moot point, isn't it? Who is right is irrelevant. In a customer-driven business, *the customer comes first*, right or wrong, informed or mistaken, polite or rude, correct or incorrect. Businesses that grasp this simple fact are the ones who will create a service advantage.

Seeing your business through the customer's glasses will require some special tools and techniques: a knowledge of *demographics* and *psychographics,* and a basic understanding of research methods and tools. This book will demystify the subject of customer perception research, show you the basic elements of it, and encourage you to start using the methods we'll describe. There are three basic questions we need to address about demographics: (1) What are they? (2) Why are they important? and (3) How do you collect them?

WHAT ARE DEMOGRAPHICS?

Demographics are among the most useful customer perception research tools at your disposal to help you begin to create a clear customer vision. Think of demographics as the vital statistics about your customers. For example, when you go out to buy some new clothes, the salesperson collects some demographic information about you: your height, weight, and your key body measurements. The salesperson still doesn't know about your likes and dislikes, your preferences for color and fabric, or design. But he or she now has the raw data to fit you with any type of clothing you might want.

Demographics are data that create factual and numerical profiles of the various segments of customers you are trying to reach with your product or service. They include information about key variables that represent the most fundamental characteristics of your customers, such as, age, sex, marital and family status, occupation, income, education, ethnicity, religion, political party, and type of housing. These types of data also tell you the size, density, and distribution of customer populations. There are probably other demographic variables that are important to your customers, depending upon what sort of business you are in.

The important thing to ask yourself is, "Do we have a clear picture of what our typical customer is like?" The demographics for customers of a college bookstore will be different from those of a customer who shops at Waldenbooks. Customer demographics for readers of *Sports Illustrated* are probably very different from those who read *Atlantic Monthly*.

Figure 5–1 illustrates a real-life example. This is a demographic profile sheet from a survey of physicians at Poudre Valley Hospital in Fort Collins, Colorado. Placed at the beginning

FIGURE 5–1
Poudre Valley Hospital Physician Survey Management Project

Demographics (Please check (✓) the following)

AGE:

A.	_____	20 - 25 yrs	F.	_____	46 - 50 yrs
B.	_____	26 - 30 yrs	G.	_____	51 - 55 yrs
C.	_____	31 - 35 yrs	H.	_____	56 - 60 yrs
D.	_____	36 - 40 yrs	I.	_____	61 - 65 yrs
E.	_____	41 - 45 yrs	J.	_____	65 yrs +

GENDER: _____ Male   _____ Female

LENGTH OF TIME AT POUDRE VALLEY HOSPITAL:

A.	_____	Less than 1 year	D.	_____	11 - 15 yrs
B.	_____	1 - 5 yrs	E.	_____	16 - 20 yrs
C.	_____	6 - 10 yrs	F.	_____	20 yrs +

SPECIALTY:

A.	_____	Cardiology	I.	_____	Orthopedics
B.	_____	Family Practice	J.	_____	Pathology
C.	_____	Gastroenterology	K.	_____	Pediatrics
D.	_____	Internal Medicine	L.	_____	Podiatry
E.	_____	Nephrology	M.	_____	Psychiatry
F.	_____	Neurosurgery	N.	_____	Radiology
G	_____	Obstetrics	O.	_____	Surgery
H.	_____	Oncology	P.	_____	Urology
			Q.	_____	Other (Please Specify)

---

of a questionnaire for the physicians who admit patients to the hospital, the demographic profile allows data from the survey to be classified according to age, gender, length of service, and specialty.

This is typical of the kinds of forms used to gather data about key customers. Your information would be different, of course, but you could use the same kind of format to create a profile of your typical customer.

Why Are Demographics Important?

Because demographics provide the profile of your average customer, they are your first source of information. These special data are the most common means for segmenting your market and for identifying new targets you wish to reach with your product or service. The demographic data you gather about your customers help answer a key question: "Who are your customers?"

Demographics are important to you because buying and consumption patterns differ widely from one demographic population to another. We noted some of these differences in chapter three when we discussed customers from the baby bust, baby boom, and traditionalist generations and their spending habits. When we compared spending patterns of teenage boys and girls in chapter two, we were citing demographic data.

While these kinds of data will be helpful to you, there will still be a need to develop specific demographic information about your customers. Customers can vary markedly. Santa Clara Medical Center in Santa Clara, California, is part of a large health maintenance organization with different facilities located within 10 miles of one another. Yet, the customers of each of them are very different, based upon available demographic data. Tom Seifert, Administrator of the Santa Clara center says, "It's not enough to know about the 'average customer' out there. We need to know about our customers in each of our clinic locations."

Do certain people use your business at one time and not at another? Are there racial, cultural, ethnic, political, geographical, or other variables that you need to know about your local customers? Getting a clear snapshot of your customer, from a demographic perspective, is one of the first tasks facing the business that wants to gain the service advantage.

How Do You Collect Demographics?

If you just need general data check out federal, state, and local census documents. They provide a lot of the demographic data used on a daily basis throughout the United States. You'll also find generally useful material in publications like *The 1989 Information Please Almanac*. A regular source of demographic data and one that is very useful, is *American Demographics* magazine, published monthly.

Many organizations have active marketing departments that can collect demographic profiles of customers. If your business doesn't have a marketing operation, you can rely on an external source for this information. There are many professional research firms whose demographers can research just about any profile data you want. But you can do much of this homework yourself.

The research methods and tools we'll discuss a bit further on and in subsequent chapters will help you collect the kind of demographic data you need to create an accurate profile of your customers. These kinds of data won't tell you why customers buy the way they do, nor will you learn about what motivates them, angers them, makes them come to see you, and makes them go away. For that information, you need psychographic data.

PSYCHOGRAPHICS

While demographic data allow you to make black and white snapshots of your typical customer, psychographic data help you create full-color movies about them. Let's consider the same three questions about psychographics: (1) What are they? (2) Why are they important? and (3) How do you collect them?

What Are Psychographics?

So far, we've focused on making a two-dimensional profile of your customer. You'll need to get into a third dimension—what makes your customers tick. What's going on in their heads at the moment of truth? What comes to mind when they think of your business? What motivates them? These are the kinds of questions designed to be answered with psychographic data.

When you want to get inside your customer's head and see how his or her mental furniture is arranged, you need psychographics. These are the data required to answer a second key question we posed earlier: "How do your customers think and feel about your product or service?" It's a more difficult question to answer than the demographics question. While many companies already have, or can get, demographic data about their customer base, not so many do a very good job of finding out what factors are critical to their customers.

The psychographic data, to a great degree, account for the critical factors on your customers' report cards. These are the significant events by which customers measure their own satisfaction with your product or service and, most importantly, they are the ways in which your business is differentiated from your competition.

At Santa Monica Hospital, management wanted to find the answers to two questions: (1) When given a choice, how many patients expressed a preference to their physicians to be admitted to a certain hospital? and (2) All things being equal, why did physicians admit patients to one hospital versus another? By interviewing physicians and following the interviews with surveying, psychographic factors were discovered that allowed the hospital to more sharply focus its marketing efforts toward physicians. Leonard LaBella, president of Santa Monica Hospital, says, "We were really surprised at the high percentage of patients who actually expressed a hospital preference to their doctors. It opened up a whole new way of thinking about the physician as a resource for patients."

Why Are Psychographics Important?

Psychographics are important because they provide you with knowledge and insight into what motivates and influences customers in their relationships with your business. Many businesses make a mistake at this point. Because of their expertise, they believe they know, in advance, what motivates their customers. They continue to follow the "we know what's best for you" paradigm and design systems and methods based upon a preconceived notion of what is best for the customer.

Customers operate at several different levels, depending upon what they want and how they go about getting what they want. The Customer Styles Model shown in Figure 5–2 is a useful way of looking at these two key dimensions.

The bottom axis represents what customers want. Some are much more oriented to the *process* than they are toward contact with *people,* that is, service employees. They are generally more interested in the way things work rather than the human relations component. Others attach more importance to the human relationship than they do to the systems. The left

FIGURE 5–2
Customer Styles Model

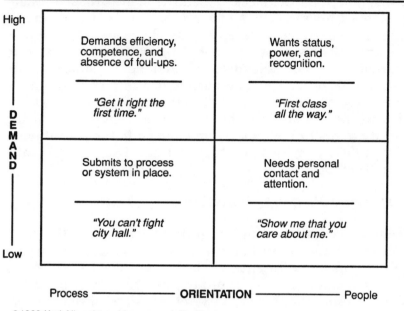

High

D
E
M
A
N
D

Low

Demands efficiency, competence, and absence of foul-ups.	Wants status, power, and recognition.
"Get it right the first time."	*"First class all the way."*
Submits to process or system in place.	Needs personal contact and attention.
"You can't fight city hall."	*"Show me that you care about me."*

Process ———————— **ORIENTATION** ———————— People

©1989 Karl Albrecht and Lawrence J. Bradford.

axis represents how customers go about getting what they want. Some customers operate at a *high demand level;* others seem to get along with *low demand levels.* By combining these elements in the model you can gain a better understanding of the general psychographics of customers.

High Demand Process Orientation

Some of your customers fall into the upper left quadrant of the model. They demand that things work right the first time and have very little tolerance for systems failures. They expect products to work, and they respect efficiency and competence. They have relatively little interest in the interpersonal relations aspects of service. As long as things work as they are supposed to, they are generally satisfied.

A favorite story illustrates the point: three prisoners were about to lose their heads on the guillotine. The first, a Frenchman, was placed on the block. When the blade dropped it suddenly stopped an inch short of his neck. The gathered crowd demanded he be freed because it was obvious that a miracle had occurred. The second prisoner, an Englishman, was led to the guillotine. The blade dropped and again stopped only inches from his neck. The crowd demanded that he too be freed because of the miraculous event. The third prisoner, a German, was led to the guillotine to have his head removed. Drawing himself up to his full height, he proclaimed to the executioner, "I refuse to place my head on the block until you fix this inferior machine!"

High Demand People Orientation

Customers that fall in this general category want the best. They expect things to work, but most importantly, they have a need for status and recognition. They want to be taken care of first. They demand and can afford to pay for the very best. The Cleveland Clinic Foundation in Cleveland is one of the first national referral centers in the United States and is an international health resource—a medical court of last resort for patients from throughout the world, principally from the Middle East, the Americas, and Europe. Some of the Clinic's patients are very affluent visitors who demand the very best in facilities for themselves and their families. In response to this need, the Clinic has constructed a VIP floor in its hospital that is furnished like a fine international hotel. Rosewood furniture, elegant carpets, expandable suites, and living quarters for traveling family members are among the special amenities for these High Demand/High People Orientation customers.

Low Demand/Process Orientation

If you have customers in this category, they likely place their trust in the systems that are in place to serve them. They tend to be compliant and believe that their needs will be adequately met if they simply allow the experts to do what they know how to do. When they are disappointed in the process they rarely complain; they just quietly go away and take their business elsewhere.

Low Demand/People Orientation

These customers are also more passive than aggressive; however, they place their trust in people rather than in systems. They need to be guided and want lots of "handholding" as they move through your organization's systems. The "low demand" aspect describes their low-key, comparatively passive behavior. They actually have a very high need for human contact and place great emphasis on how they are treated interpersonally.

A similar typography has been developed by SAS International Hotels, a division of the Scandinavian Airline Systems. Each of SAS' 21 wholly owned hotels operates in the upscale end of the market, where customers are affluent and very demanding. "We can't afford to mess up with them, and whenever we do, we go to great lengths to make it up to them," says Christian Sinding, vice president for the SAS Hotels division. "We work very hard to capture and keep their business."

Sinding and his executives think and talk in terms of two kinds of customers: the Late Majority and the Early Majority. These categories are similar to those described in Chapter 3: "Anatomy of the Service Customer of the 1990s". According to Sinding, "The Late Majority category tends to be older, and consists of the Tradition Oriented and the Sociocentric people. Traditionalists value reliability in the product, security, and sensible thinking. Sociocentric people want human interaction, personal attention, and confirmation of their values." Sinding believes the Late Majority account for about 70 percent of hotel customers.

"The Early Majority," Sinding continues, "are either Efficiency Oriented or Status Oriented. The Efficiency Oriented are quality conscious, results oriented, and intolerant of failure or incompetence. The Status Oriented are prestige conscious, identity-seeking, and very demanding of personal deference." He believes the Early Majority makes up about 30 percent of SAS Hotels' business.

This viewpoint about customers and the key attributes they value in the hotel experience, translates into decision criteria concerning the service product. "For example," says Sinding, "an executive floor or concierge-type floor appeals very strongly to certain categories of customers but not so much to others. Business service centers are right for some types but not for others. Express check-in and check-out might appeal to the Efficiency Oriented Early Majority, but the Sociocentric person in the Late Majority category might value the human contact at the counter and not be concerned about the waiting time."

When psychographic information such as that shown in the Customer Styles Model in Figure 5–2 are ignored you can make costly mistakes, as Jan Carlzon, president of Scandinavian Airline Systems, discovered.

Before he took over the helm of SAS, Carlzon was the 32 year-old president of Vingresor, a subsidiary of SAS, which specialized in arranging and selling packaged vacation tours. Carlzon and his management group decided that Swedish senior citizens would be likely customers for a new tour package designed especially for older travelers.

> We . . . concluded that senior citizens were fearful of traveling abroad and therefore would want to stay in special hotels filled only with other Swedish senior citizens. We knew the tour conductors should be solid, down-to-earth people—probably ruddy-cheeked, matronly nurses. We arranged a wealth of brief excursions, interspersed with plenty of restroom breaks.

Carlzon and his management group then decided to find out what a group of senior citizens thought about the idea and invited a group of 15 from a Stockholm retirement club to Vingresor headquarters to discuss it. What they found out was that not one of the seniors thought the package was a good idea, and it was contrary to the kind of vacation they wanted.

> And so it continued, until finally not a single retiree there expressed interest in our wonderful product. We thanked them for coming to Vingresor and promptly dismissed all of their opinions. We stubbornly invested $100,000 in beautiful, tabloid-size brochures. And our matronly nurses were left waiting for pensioners who never showed up. That's what happens when you sit

at the top of the pyramid, far from the reality of the market, and you develop a product you think will please your customers.[1]

Psychographic data are important because they are the only means through which you can truly come to know your customer, as Carlzon learned from his expensive lesson. Additionally, they are important because they can help you discover key factors on your customer's report cards that you might never have thought existed.

The first hospital in the country to do a full implementation of service management was Santa Monica Hospital in Santa Monica, California. Through focus groups and follow-up surveys with patients, we discovered a piece of psychographic data that proved to be very important in the hospital's program to become service-driven. Patients didn't have a very high level of trust and confidence in hospitals in general. While Santa Monica had good demographic data about its customers, the information about the psychographics was less clear. The hospital included this factor as part of a carefully orchestrated service implementation effort.

How Do You Collect Psychographics?

Psychographic data are collected primarily through face-to-face interviews and focus groups, followed by telephone or written surveys and questionnaires. It is important to remember that focus groups and interviews only help you surface *potential* factors on your customers' report cards. You still need to verify that what a small group of people has told you holds true for a representative sample of your customer population.

You can obtain generalized psychographic data about typical customers of your product or service from market profiles. Commercial services are available, such as the Yankelovich Monitor service. In operation since 1970, the annual "Monitor" surveys 2,500 American adults. Over 100 business firms and organizations participate and sponsor the service at an initial cost of $2,500 for the first year of participation. The Yankelovich Monitor measures over 40 different social trends.[2] Your professional associations and societies may be sources for such information as well.

Let's take a look at some simple research methods to help you get the information you need about your customers. Many people cringe when you say the word, "research." Don't be put off. You don't need to understand deep applications of statistics to get the data you need. A basic comprehension of the tools and techniques will get you well on your way.

RESEARCH METHODS

There are two major approaches used to research the critical factors on your customers' report cards: *qualitative* and *quantitative* methods. We can get a better understanding of the difference between these two by comparing them to something simple. When you go to the market to shop for some fresh fruit, you use both approaches. First, your brain uses the *qualitative* approach. You see the cantaloupe. You notice its color. You pick it up and squeeze it. You smell it. You heft it a bit in your hand. You look at the name of the brand. You ask the produce manager if it is fresh. Then your brain shifts to the *quantitative* method. You check the price per pound. You pick up three cantaloupes and place them on the scale. You calculate in your head how much they will cost, based on the price per pound. It's that simple. Qualitative data tell you the *subjective aspects* of the cantaloupe: color, smell, and perceived freshness. Quantitative data tell you the *objective aspects* such as cost, price, and weight. The former is a function of your perception or someone else's opinion. The latter can be verified and measured with numbers.

We'll have a lot more to say about these in subsequent chapters. For now, here's a brief introduction to using these powerful customer perception research techniques to help you look through your customers' glasses.

Qualitative Methods

Simply put, qualitative methods allow you to assess how your customer organizes his or her world. Qualitative methods let you look through the customer's glasses. The kinds of data generated through qualitative methods are rarely conclusive. They're not used to prove anything statistically. By definition, these data are heavily filtered and colored by the person giving the information (the produce manager *says* the cantaloupes are fresh). The importance of understanding the notion of frame of reference needs to be reiterated here. With qualitative methods you can get inside the customer's frame of reference. You'll be able to get a clearer picture of his or her values, expectations, and so forth. *But, it is essential that you explore the customer's perspective from his or her frame of reference.* You must accept their particular view of the world. Even if it doesn't seem to make sense to you, it makes sense to them.

Quantitative Methods

The easiest way to remember this type of research method is to think of the word, "quantity." These techniques measure *quantities.* The use of statistical measurement allows you to verify, with representative samples, the subjective trends and factors that emerge in the qualitative research. When using quantitative methods you use properly designed and executed surveys and questionnaires.

This is another point at which many businesses make a mistake. The genuine need to obtain valid and reliable information overrides the need to see through their customers' eyes. Often, an executive or manager who wants market information will skip the qualitative methods and jump right into designing a survey or questionnaire. This usually produces statistically valid and reliable results, but still doesn't reveal very much about the customer's frame of reference. We recommend you begin with the qualitative methods and then use the quantitative methods to verify if what you find out with your customers face-to-face holds true for a representative sample of them.

Research Tools

There are numerous ways to gather qualitative and quantitative data. Among the most common qualitative research tools are: face-to-face in-depth interviews, opportunistic interviews, telephone interviews, on-site interviews, and focus group interviews. While there are numerous quantitative tools for measuring your customer report cards, surveys—written and telephone—and questionnaires are the ones you'll use most frequently. You will learn how to use all of these tools in chapters seven and eight. But there is much homework you can do right now to get to know your customer better. That's the focus for the next chapter.

NOTES

1. Jan Carlzon, *Moments of Truth* (Cambridge, Mass: Ballinger, 1987), p. 44.
2. Robert B. Settle and Pamela L. Alreck, *Why They Buy: American Consumers Inside and Out* (New York: John Wiley & Sons, Inc., 1986), pp. 272–73.

CHAPTER 6

START WITH THE OBVIOUS

"Getting to know you . . ."

In Rogers and Hammerstein's famous musical, *The King and I,* Anna, the teacher, sings to the king's many children, "Getting to know you, getting to know all about you. Getting to like you, getting to hope you like me." That's what we mean when we suggest starting with the obvious. What can you do, now, to get to know your customer?

WHAT'S GOING ON INSIDE?

First, look within. Your employees should be your first market in any service initiative. One of the lessons we've learned in working with companies that wish to become service-driven is that if you haven't sold your employees on the notion of superior service it will be very difficult, if not impossible, to change the organizational culture to one that puts the customer first. It is a serious mistake to attempt to launch a service initiative in an organization which has internal problems or issues that may be counterproductive to the new service culture.

If you haven't done an assessment of the internal climate of your business, this is your first step. You have to discover whether or not the organization is ready for a major cultural change. In organization development parlance we call this "organizational readiness." We've taken a valuable lesson from the medical care professions: "Prescription without diagnosis is malpractice, whether it's medicine or management."

THE EMPLOYEE: YOUR FRONTLINE RADAR

Your employees represent one of your most valuable means for gathering information about your customers. Think of them as a sort of frontline radar; an early warning system. Your business probably has more "radar stations" than you know. And each of them can function as a valuable data collection center.

The employee can serve as an on-the-spot market researcher. Who is in a better position to evaluate the customer's experience than the person who is involved in it at the moment of truth? A word of caution: don't let your service employee fall into a routinized, "Is everything OK?" trap. When they do, they aren't really prepared to listen to the customer and to do something that will fix the customer's problem. Has something like the following happened to you?

After a meal in a restaurant where the service was slow and surly, and the food was improperly cooked, you approach the cashier to pay your bill. "How was everything this morning?" the cashier chirps, in a most cheerful voice. You relay that the service was poor and the food was not cooked properly. After giving you a blank look for a few seconds, the cashier slips back into a rehearsed routine, flashes a bright smile and says, "Have a nice day!" Sound familiar?

Your employees can be your best secret weapon in the war to win customers if you show them how to do on-the-spot market research. Encourage them to ask a few well-placed questions:

"Were you satisfied with your shopping experience in my department today?"

"Was there anything that caused a problem for you in visiting our store this morning?"

"Is there any message you'd like me to pass on to our manager for you?"

These questions must then be followed by careful, active listening, a skill which many employees have never learned. If your employees aren't actively listening to customers, you're missing a vital link in the service chain. When an employee listens actively he or she pays attention to all the signals coming from customers. Signals like facial expression, tone of voice, gestures, body posture, and eye contact are every bit as important as the actual content of the customer's words.

Other radar stations for gathering customer information are at refund and exchange counters. Often these are the best opportunities to learn about customers' buying habits. The customer must not feel that he or she is getting interrogated as a condition for getting a refund or exchange. Have employees ask some key questions *after* they have made the refund or exchange:

> "We want to do our best for you. Could you tell me why this merchandise didn't suit you?"
>
> "Was there anything we could have done better in serving you?"
>
> "Did you get the help you needed when you selected this particular product?"

Of course, if your business doesn't produce a tangible product that is subject to point of purchase, refund, or exchange, you will have a different set of radar stations. Take a good, hard look around the organization. What would be the most likely locations for doing on-the-spot market research by employees?

Customer Contact Employees

In a service-driven business, everyone is responsible for managing service. But there is a special category of persons who are ideally placed to help you get to know your customer better: your customer contact employees.

These are the men and women whose jobs place them into regular face-to-face encounters with customers on a daily basis. In most instances they are frontline people. In a retail store, salespersons, security guards, receptionists, credit department, gift wrap, and return and exchange personnel come to mind. A medical setting, such as a hospital, would include volunteers, technicians, doctors, nurses, housekeepers, and business office representatives. A restaurant has waiters and waitresses, bussers, car valets, coat check, wine experts, and entertainment personnel. A hotel would count bellpersons, desk clerks, gift shop salespersons, room service people, maids, and restaurant and bar personnel in the customer contact category.

Each of these persons, irrespective of the kind of business you are in, can serve as a magnet to attract information about the customer. How well are you using these resources? Who are the customer contact people in your business? It's a sad fact that many customer-contact employees are among the poorest trained and lowest paid personnel in a business. And they are the ones who man the frontline radar stations!

We've mentioned Nordstrom, the northwest based retail store chain with a national reputation for superior service. Nordstrom places such a premium on customer information that it bases many of its merchandise buying priorities on what salespeople tell them, not what buyers think will be big demand items. Nordstrom's frontline people, the sales associates, work on commission, and they listen carefully to their customers to find out what they want.

Disneyland discovered something interesting from its frontline employees. The company decided to run a promotion in which random visitors to the amusement park would be chosen to receive prizes. The response was positive, and a major campaign was designed around the idea. At the entrance to Disneyland was a large neon sign proclaiming, "The Happiest Place On Earth." As a part of this campaign, the sign was changed to "Where There's a Winner Every Day!" Employees rose up in unison to oppose this change. They had been steeped in the Disney tradition of providing happiness as a product to their customers. "We're not a casino!" they protested. Disneyland executives listened to their employees and changed the sign back to "The Happiest Place On Earth."

THE EMPLOYEE AS CUSTOMER ADVOCATE

We say, "start with the obvious" in your quest to understand customer perceptions. But we know the obvious is often the most overlooked. For example, who, in your business, is an advocate for the customer? If your organization is like many others, there's virtually no one who has been made the customer's ombudsman. Our bias is toward making every employee a customer advocate. When employees take customers under their wings and see that the customer's problem is solved, you open the door to a good deal of important information about the buyer of your service or product. Most service encounters are brief, a few minutes at best. If employees start functioning as customer advocates, a new sense of responsibility for knowing those customers inside and out begins to take place in the employees' minds.

A customer advocate goes beyond providing a service or product to the customer. A personal relationship with the customer gets established. As customers become known on a more intimate basis their trust grows. And their willingness to express their concerns, wishes, and preferences will increase. When the customer believes that the service encounter is a one-time spin around the dance floor, he or she is less willing to take the time to provide the valuable information which you need to know.

Becoming a customer advocate will require special attention to orienting new employees and to training existing ones. When employees are recognized and rewarded for going out of their way to represent the customer, then advocacy grows. Employees must be given the authority to solve customer problems at their own level and to help customers make it through the organization's systems with as little pain and suffering as possible.

THE CUSTOMER IS ALWAYS TELLING YOU

Are you listening? Customers constantly tell you what they think. They do it in subtle and not so subtle ways. Communicologists tell us that more then 55 percent of the meaning of a person's communication is revealed by nonverbal language, that is, facial expression, gestures, posture, and tone of voice. Take time to watch your customers from a distance. Notice how they approach the moment of truth encounter. What emotional state do they bring with them? We don't want to oversimplify psychology, but most people will approach the moment of truth with one of four mental and emotional states: mad, sad, glad, or scared.

"I'm mad . . ."

The angry customer is well known. They have a gripe about your product or service and they are going to tell you about it in clear, down-to-earth language. This is a moment of truth for the person who encounters this customer, whether he or she had anything to do with the problem or not.

The problem with anger is that it can be extremely contagious. If you or your service employee allow yourselves to get "hooked" by the customers' anger, then you won't be able to really listen to them. All of your personnel should know how to manage anger, both their own and that of others whom they encounter during the many moments of truth that occur in your business.

"I'm sad . . ."

This customer is talking to you, too. He or she has been disappointed. By listening to the complaint, you can track down that part of the system that has failed to satisfy your customer. The sad or depressed customer is found frequently in medical settings. They are the sick and injured, or the family members of those who are. Service employees who must routinely work with saddened customers need special training and insights to manage these special moments of truth.

"I'm glad . . ."

Of course, you wish all your customers were glad, all the time. Often, however, we fail to listen to the satisfied customer. If your focus becomes centered on the ones who got away or who are about to, you may forget about retaining the customers you have. A big part of listening to customers is to discover what you're doing right and to continue doing it. It's been clearly established that it is much easier to keep the customers you have than it is to go out and get new ones. It's surprising how many businesses take their "glad" customers for granted. What are you doing, on a regular basis, to keep them in that "glad" category?

"I'm scared . . ."
When the customer's emotional state is one of fear, special
handling is required. Fear is most often a belief or concern that
something precious is at risk or is going to be lost. The fear of
uncertainty, of pain, of financial commitment, or fear for one's
welfare are all possible inputs which contribute to the scared
customer's frame of reference. Children are often the customers who fit this category when they face something scary to
them, for example, the dentist or the school nurse with a sy-
ringe and needle in hand.

Elderly persons on fixed incomes who see their utility bills
increasing often experience fear as a driving input. The skill
with which customer service representatives handle this special category of customer is crucial. Public Service Company of
Colorado, a gas and electric utility headquartered in Denver,
has taken the lead in this area by establishing personal account representatives to work with indigent customers to help
them manage their utility bills. The company also established
a program to match contributions from customers to help indigent consumers pay their utility bills.

One of the most important facts to know is that human
beings can shift from one emotional state to another very
quickly. Consider how the average customer approaches your
business. Assuming there is no immediate problem, the customer probably approaches the moment of truth with an air of
expectation. They are not mad, not scared, and not sad. There
is probably a sense of anticipation, of gladness, and the belief
that a pleasant experience is about to occur.

How Quickly They Can Change
The customer's state of mind can change quickly when con-
fronted by someone who doesn't listen. The "glad" customer
can change to the "mad" customer in front of your eyes. Lee
Hogan, a management consultant in Denver, told of an instance in which he wanted to purchase a typewriter for his
daughter's high school graduation present. He was excited and
happy about surprising her with this useful gift to take away
to college. "I explained to the sales clerk the kind of typewriter
I wanted and why. He completely ignored what I told him and
proceeded to try to bump me up to a personal computer, which

my daughter neither wanted nor needed. In spite of several attempts to convince him that I just wanted to buy a plain, electric typewriter, he persisted. I started to get mad. I was frustrated because this person apparently was unwilling or unable to listen to me. Finally, I told him, 'To hell with it' and left the store. I'd never go back there again."

In the same way, the sad, mad, or scared customer can often be changed to a glad one if you take the time to really listen to what is being said. The ability of everyone in your organization to pick up the ball when it has been fumbled and to make your customers feel as though someone is truly interested in what they have to say can pay long-term dividends.

CUSTOMER SERVICE DEPARTMENTS

If you have sensitive toes, beware. We may step on them now. Customer service departments are, in many instances, contradictions in terms. What should be one of your prime radar stations for gathering customer information is often nothing more than an entry-level position with little or no training and poor pay. These departments are sometimes populated by employees who lack essential interpersonal skills, with the result that the customer gets treated poorly. It's almost as though the departments have been set up as a court in which the customer must prove his or her case before being offered any assistance.

Another problem with customer service departments (CSD) is that too often they represent a box on some organization's chart. When you have a CSD it may not be a good sign. It's often a signal to workers that "the company is being taken care of and you can go on about your business." A mixed message can go out through the company that if there are any problems with customers, send them on to the customer service department. That effectively relieves everyone but the customer service representatives of any responsibility for managing moments of truth and, ultimately, the quality of service. Why should any employee become an advocate for the customer when the organization has designated an official repository for customer problems?

Customer service departments can be very useful to the organization and helpful to the customer. But the people who work there must be of the caliber who can make decisions on the spot to solve the customer's problems. That means that management must empower them with responsibility.

Our bias, if you haven't guessed it by now, is toward making the entire organization one gigantic customer service department. Make every person responsible for managing service and for listening to the customer. When that happens, the customer service department joins other radar stations as sources of valuable information about the buyer.

MANAGEMENT'S PERSONAL RADAR

Tom Peters made MBWA (management by walking around) a business buzzword. But just walking around won't get the job done in a service-managed business. Executives and managers who want to create a customer-driven climate must get to know their customers—up close and personal. In *In Search of Excellence* Peters and Waterman noted, "The excellent companies really are close to their customers. That's it. Other companies talk about it; the excellent companies do it. They do seem to us more driven by their direct orientation to their customers than by technology or by a desire to be the low-cost producer."[1]

How can management get close to the customer? It won't happen if executives and managers stay closed in their offices. The downside of someone who rises in management positions is that he or she gets further and further away from direct contact with the customer. You have to discover ways of getting managers back in contact with customers. Here's how one company is doing it.

Santa Clara Medical Center in Santa Clara, California, is a large Kaiser Permanente hospital and clinic. Tom Seifert, administrator, instituted a program to get managers closer to customers. The program is called, "Managers on the Move" (MOM), and is strictly voluntary. Each manager can volunteer a three-hour block in his or her work day to be a MOM. The manager's job as a MOM is to roam throughout the hospital, meeting patients, conversing with employees, and solving problems. What makes the program unique is that the MOM on duty has discretionary authority to solve most problems on the spot. No red tape. No forms to fill out. The program has been a tremendous success, with more than 90 percent of the management staff volunteering for MOM duty. Letters from patients support the popularity of the program.

At Poudre Valley Hospital in Ft. Collins, Colorado, managers "make rounds", that is, they spend time visiting with patients and circulate throughout the medical center.

These are the kinds of programs that will help managers get into closer contact with customers. The opportunities to glean valuable customer information are extraordinary. The Santa Clara MOM program has resulted in more than 100 service improvements, due largely to feedback to managers who are in direct contact with customers.

Take a look around your business. Are you capitalizing upon the obvious opportunities to get to know your customers? Are you and your service personnel really listening to the customer? Have employees been used effectively as information gathering stations about customer problems and preferences? Is your customer service department really an advocate for the customer? And when was the last time you or your managers spent time out in the field, on the floor, or in the store, "making rounds?"

NOTE

1. Thomas J. Peters and Robert H. Waterman, Jr., *In Search of Excellence: Lessons from America's Best-Run Companies,* (New York: Harper & Row, 1982), pp. 156–57.

CHAPTER 7

THE FACE TO FACE
ADVANTAGE

The advantage of being able to talk face-to-face with your clients is that the whole menu of human response is open to you. Unlike the telephone or written survey, you can watch the respondent's reactions to your questions. You can see when the brow furrows and the face frowns. The intensity of feelings about the important service attributes in the customer's experience can be assessed in a way that pencil and paper surveys cannot. An additional advantage is that you come to see your customers as individuals, each bringing their own preferences and expectations to your business. Meeting and talking to your customers one-on-one or in small groups creates the kind of rich qualitative data that really help you identify their needs as they perceive them.

INTERVIEW YOUR CUSTOMERS

Interviewing your customers is the most basic kind of qualitative research you can do if you want to get close to them. The inherent advantage in interview research is that you have a warm, live, breathing customer whose perceptions can be checked on-the-spot. The immediacy of the various kinds of interview research produces rich data. We aren't denigrating quantitative methods or tools at all. In fact, you will need to use them to verify what you find out in the interviews. As rich as the perspectives are that you get from interview research, rarely can you generalize the feelings and experiences of a handful of customers to all of your customers. That is where the quantitative methods come into play and must be put to use. The best starting point in getting to know your customers, in our opinion, is by using interviews of various types to discover what's on their minds. Let's take a closer look at these types of interviews: depth, intercept, opportunistic, telephone, on-site, and focus-group.

DEPTH INTERVIEWS

Depth interviews are just what their name suggests. They are interviews between you and one or two of your customers at a time, during which you explore all the aspects of your product or service *in depth*. They take longer than most of the other types because of the time required to develop the discussion.

There are a couple of good reasons to use depth interviews as your starting point: one is if you are inexperienced at doing customer perception research; and the other is if most of your customer information in the past has come only from surveys and questionnaires. In the first instance, doing depth interviews with one or two people at a time is less threatening, both to you and to the persons being interviewed. You'll gain a lot of skills as you practice talking with your customers. Secondly, the depth interview will allow you to explore your service product in detail, something a questionnaire just can't do.

When conducting depth interviews, select a few individuals or families, if you wish, and invite them to participate in an extended discussion of your product or service. Let them know that you will need up to two or three hours to complete the interview. Northwestern Mutual Life Insurance Co. has been doing this every year since 1907. The company invites five policy owners to corporate headquarters in Milwaukee to participate in depth interviews over a five-day period with Northwestern managers and executives. Donald Schuenke, chief executive officer, says, "This is good for us. It really helps to keep us on our toes."[1]

You may not want to spend five days talking to your customers, but setting aside several hours can really pay dividends. Here's another example: when General Motors' (GM) designers chopped two feet off the 1984 Cadillac, sales stalled. GM decided to take a new approach before they fiddled with the car's design again. Company interviewers met with 500 owners of Cadillacs over a three-year period to discuss design ideas. They covered every detail of the Cadillac, from the owners' perspectives, asking, in effect, "How do you want your Cadillac to be built?" The result was that in 1988 Cadillac sales leaped 36 percent over the previous year and for the first time in five years, sales are growing in volume. John Fleming, director of marketing and planning, says, "We learned a very tough lesson. We learned to pay great attention to the customer."[2]

Depth interviews will help you develop the key attributes on your customer report cards. The technique itself is very simple. Start with some broad questions, for example, "What's it like to do business at our store?" or "When you come here to shop, what really bugs you?" Then practice those active listening skills we mentioned earlier and tune into your customers. You'll find that after you interview several customers, repetitive points of discussion will emerge. These are *critical incidents* and they deserve special attention. Further on, when we explain surveys and questionnaires, we'll tell you how to use the critical incidents.

INTERCEPT INTERVIEWS

There are numerous opportunities to interview customers that are overlooked every day. We call these "intercept interviews." They are encounters with customers that are good points at which to check the perception of the quality of your service. A customer service desk is an excellent location for intercept interviewing. Some retail stores offer an immediate incentive, such as a 10 percent discount, in return for answering a few questions at the customer service desk.

Depending upon the nature of your business, you could post an employee near the entrance of your store or office and conduct brief "exit" interviews with customers. You could offer a coupon for a future discount as an incentive to participate in an interview.

Special stations can be set up where customers have to spend time waiting. For example, if there is a location in your business where customers must wait in line or in a reception area, that may be a good spot for an intercept interview.

In addition to locations, certain events are naturals for these kinds of interviews. Points at which bills are paid, complaints are made, and where merchandise is exchanged are all likely events.

Intercept interviews should be brief—not more than five minutes or so. Each should be carefully structured with three or four key questions to ask the customer. Persons who conduct this type of interview should be friendly and comfortable in establishing rapport quickly with strangers. Don't select unassertive, shy, or overly aggressive employees to conduct these interviews.

Each interview should have a beginning, a middle, and an end. The beginning is the approach, or rapport building statement: "Hello, I'm Mary Brown. I work for Super Stores. I wonder if you could answer a few questions about your shopping experience today?" The middle of the interview is where the actual questions get asked. The end of the interview summarizes the customer's opinions and offers an opportunity for any other comments or questions the customer may have. Then the reward or incentive is presented, and the customer is thanked for his or her help.

British Airways has for a number of years employed intercept interviews in airports. Interviewers stop people and ask them to respond to a series of questions, and also solicit unstructured feedback on their travel experiences. This unstructured feedback is often more valuable than the statistical measures of satisfaction, because it illuminates aspects of customer experience that airline employees and managers may have overlooked.

OPPORTUNITY INTERVIEWS

Opportunity interviews are very similar to intercept interviews in that they attempt to sample customer opinion on-the-spot. The difference is that the opportunity interview happens during the moment of truth encounter, whereas the intercept interview more often happens after the cycle of service has been completed.

These types of interviews are less structured than the intercept interviews. They are quick perception-checks with the customers as to the quality of their service experience. The service employee asks brief questions during the service cycle, and customers express their immediate opinion of the quality of service.

A familiar opportunity interview happens in restaurant settings. A few minutes after your meal has been served the waiter or waitress might come by your table to inquire, "Is everything all right?" A better question would be, "Is your food prepared the way you like it?" If you wanted to check on the quality of service, you would ask, "Is the service you're receiving satisfactory? Is everyone doing his or her job to your satisfaction?"

In a retail setting, a customer who is looking for clothing is often asked by a sales person, "Do you need any help?" A better opportunity interview question would be, "Are you having any problem finding what you need?" Another might be, "How do you like the way this merchandise is displayed?" Or, "Has anyone offered to help you find what you need?"

A good deal of excellent information about your customer is lost because frontline employees do not capture the information obtained in opportunity interviews. More often than not, their questions are simply habitual inquiries, and none of the valuable customer input is captured and used for service improvement. Give employees an incentive for writing down and reporting customer input that is obtained during the moment of truth encounter. Provide all employees with questions to ask on a regular basis as they encounter customers at key points in the various cycles of service.

TELEPHONE INTERVIEWS

Interviewing customers by telephone has several inherent advantages. Interviewers can follow a script to ensure that each customer is asked the same questions in the same way. The technology supporting telephone interviews can save a tremendous amount of research time. Automatic dialers and computer-driven systems help reach a large number of people in a relatively short time. One of the current trends is toward computer interviews in which the respondent replies by punching a button on the telephone in response to questions.

We prefer face-to-face interviews because of the reasons stated earlier. However, the telephone interview can be a very efficient way to stay on top of consumer perceptions about your business.

A twist on telephone interviewing is to provide time for employees to call customers whom they have served. Let's say you've purchased a TV, and the salesperson from whom you purchased the set calls to be sure the set is working properly, and that you are happy with the purchase. "While I have you on the phone" he or she might say, "would you mind answering a few other questions about your experience in our store?" This is opportunity interviewing by telephone.

If you intend for the telephone interviews to provide you with data for decision making about customers, you need to pay attention to some of the requirements explained in Chapter Eight about random selection, validity, and reliability. You will need to be sure your telephone interviews are randomly selected and conducted in such a way as to control response bias.

The disadvantage of telephone interviewing is that you miss the nonverbal communication possible when you are face-to-face with the customer. Sometimes, what a person reveals with nonverbal signals says as much or more than the words used.

ON-SITE INTERVIEWS

There are two sites where face-to-face interviews can occur: at your business or at the customer's location. There are advantages and disadvantages to each. One of the advantages of interviewing at the customers' location is their convenience. Most customers appreciate your extra effort to come to them.

Another advantage of interviewing at the customer's site is that you can gain additional information about the customer that you might not have obtained before. Visiting the customers in their own surroundings can provide additional insights as to their values, attitudes, and beliefs.

The disadvantage of interviewing on-site is that of time spent and distance traveled. Both add to the cost of conducting customer perception research. The advantage of bringing customers to your site for interviews is one of efficiency. Also, interviewing on your own site allows you to control time better than when you are at the customer's location.

Whether you sample customer opinion on-site, at their location, or in your own business setting, you will need to do two types of interviews: depth and focus group. The techniques we've described so far lend themselves more to the one-on-one, in-depth format. The next section describes how to conduct focus groups to obtain customer information. Because focus groups are the fundamental tool of market research and testing customer opinion, we will discuss them in greater detail.

FOCUS GROUP INTERVIEWS

The focus group can be a powerful and useful way to discover the critical factors that appear on your customers' report cards. Long used in qualitative research to discover how people view events and the world around them, focus groups can be a very useful way to take a look at your organization's product or service through the eyes of your customer.

Case in point: When Motorola conducted focus groups with its customers, complaints that the company was hard to do business with began to emerge. Chairman of the company, Robert Galvin, decided to make "total customer satisfaction" the focus for Motorola's 1988 Senior Executive Program, an annual conference for 200 of the firm's top executives. Kenneth Hussler, senior vice president says, "What emerged from all the meetings was the realization that we had lost something. We were being driven by cost saving instead of taking care of the customer."[3]

Here's an example from an unlikely source, the Internal Revenue Service. When it came time to redesign the 1988 income tax forms, the IRS made use of focus groups. The IRS tax form designers drafted new forms to overcome some of the monumental problems caused by the 1987 forms. They then spent the summer of 1988 crisscrossing the country, observing 62 focus groups in which 8 to 10 men and women tried out the new tax forms. "It made us a little more sensitive to the struggling over the kitchen table," said one IRS official.[4] We weren't asked, but had we been, we probably would've suggested that the IRS do some depth interviews or focus group research first, to find out what taxpayers found difficult about the old forms before drafting new ones.

When you conduct focus group interviews, you're looking for the first answers to the most important question you can ask about your customers: "How does the customer think and feel about our product or service?"

Why Conduct Focus Groups?

Why not just construct a survey or questionnaire and send it out to a randomly selected group of customers? Many businesses do just that. There's nothing inherently wrong with this approach. If it is properly designed, you will receive valid and reliable information about your customers. The only reservation we have is that often such questionnaires and surveys don't provide for the customer's perception of what is important. If you construct a survey that represents only what you, the business owner want to know, you may miss some part of your customer's frame of reference that is extremely important.

Also, because your customers are constantly changing, so are their behaviors. The questions you asked on last year's customer satisfaction survey may no longer be relevant this year. New issues and concerns may have developed that you can only discover by talking face-to-face with your customers.

What Do They Tell You?

Focus groups tell you what a small, nonscientific sample of your customers think of your product and service. You cannot generalize to all your customers on the basis of focus groups, but you will begin to discover the critical factors that are of importance to them. Focus groups allow you to discover rich, qualitative data that purely quantitative research cannot, by its nature, discover. As a result, your surveys and questionnaires will be certain to cover those items that are of interest and concern to your customers. You can always add the questions you want to ask, if they don't turn up as critical factors from your focus groups.

Recruiting the Focus Group

Your focus groups can be recruited in a couple of different ways. One way is to simply ask for volunteers from the population you wish to interview. At San Bernardino Community Hospital in San Bernardino, California, the executive team decided they wanted three surveys: physicians, hospital employees, and patients. Each doctor received a letter from Robert Lund, the president of the hospital, explaining the project and inviting him or her to participate. Depth interviews were then conducted with physicians who agreed to participate.

The second set of focus groups was with hospital employees. A second letter went out to all employees from Lund, explaining the importance of excellent service to the hospital and asking employees to share their perceptions of the quality of service provided to customers. The employees were segmented by specialty departments and by shift. Volunteers were recruited for each of six focus groups.

The third population to participate were customers of the hospital—patients. These groups were selected by the hospital's organization development group and represented a cross section of current and previous patients, medical and surgical patients, and family members of patients treated at the hospital. Again, a special letter from the president of the hospital explained the project and invited patients to participate in the focus groups. We strongly recommend that the president or other senior executive send the invitation letter. It is important that your customers perceive that the organization is very serious about getting their opinions and the endorsement of the senior executive demonstrates a personal commitment to the project. Figure 7-1 is an example of a letter inviting customers to participate in focus groups that you could easily adapt and use.

Another way to recruit focus groups is to use a research or marketing firm to select a cross section of your customers. When you invite customers to participate in a focus group, be prepared to pay each of them an honorarium, as noted in our sample letter. The going rate is about $25 at the low end and $75 at the high end. These interviews usually require one to two hours, and you may want to provide refreshments for the participants. Focus groups can be conducted on your premises or at a meeting room in a local hotel or community center. Try to make it as convenient as possible for the volunteers, both in terms of location and time of day.

Focus groups are also very useful for assessing the organizational climate. Public Service Company of Colorado wanted to assess the work climate of supervisors and employees in its large customer service group. Through focus groups with supervisors and employees, many key issues were discovered to guide the company's decision making in the customer service area. Gregory Thielen, manager of customer service, says, "The focus groups allowed us to identify some of the really important issues with our supervisors and customer service employees."

FIGURE 7–1

XYZ Corporation
Your Address
Your City and State   Office of the President

Date
Inside Address

Dear Mr. Customer,

As part of our continuing effort to improve the
quality of service we provide to you, our customers, we
are implementing a program to make XYZ Corporation
totally customer-focused, with superior service as our
driving force.

Mr. Customer, <u>you are the most important part of
this effort.</u>   I'd like to invite you to participate in a
small group discussion where you can tell us, frankly and
honestly, how we're doing on your score card.   You will
be part of a group of about eight other customers whose
names were randomly selected, like yours. You will be
interviewed by a member of a research firm we've retained
for this project.

The time required is minimal—about an hour or
so—and your input is extremely important to us. Your
comments will help paint a good picture of our current
level of service—where it's working and ways it can be
improved.

I want to prove how much we value your opinion.
Each participant in our focus groups will receive a
crisp, new $50 bill at the end of the interview.

Our customer service manager, Ms. Jones, will be
calling you next week to see if you can help us out.
Thank you very much, in advance, for your participation.

Cordially,

Sharon Persons
President

How Many Focus Groups Do You Need?

This is one of those, "How long is a piece of string?" questions. It is important to remember that with focus groups you are not necessarily seeking statistical validity. That is, you're not trying to reach conclusions about most of your customers based upon the experiences of a few. Instead, you're trying to discover all the key buying issues. With that in mind, you need enough focus groups to assure that you've sampled a good cross section of the population you want to survey, to make sure all of the critical incidents will emerge.

San Bernardino Community Hospital in San Bernardino, California conducted five focus groups of patients, grouping them by treatment received (e.g., surgical, medical, etc.). It all really depends on the breadth and depth of your customer base. If you have customers spread throughout North America, or abroad, you will probably want to conduct focus groups in each of your major company locations.

We recommend that a basic number of focus groups be chosen to start, say five or six groups. If you continue to uncover new emergent themes, then add one or two more groups until you no longer hear any new information. Keep in mind that geographical differences, age, gender, and so forth, are segmenting factors, all of which affect the number and type of focus groups you may wish to conduct.

How many people should be in each focus group? The minimum is 5 and the maximum is about 10. The answer is somewhat dependent upon who is doing the interviews. One interviewer is more efficient, but can handle fewer people. If you can, use two interviewers with each group. One interviewer asks questions and the second records answers. They usually switch roles from group to group. With two interviewers you can handle larger focus groups.

Preparing For Focus Group Interviews

Focus group interviews are much less structured than telephone interviews, which, of necessity, must be carefully scripted. There are at least two schools of thought on this. One school holds that an interview protocol should be developed for the focus groups and followed religiously by the interviewer. The second school believes that interviews in focus groups should be completely unstructured so that the subjects of importance to the customers will emerge naturally.

Our approach is a hybrid of both. We prepare for the focus group interviews by finding out as much as possible about the people who will participate. This is not always possible, especially if the participants have been randomly selected by an outside firm. We always have a set of "guide questions" that we want to be sure to cover with each group. Often these are questions that our client wants specifically to have explored. But we also keep the interviews fairly unstructured and free flowing. When customers are allowed to talk about what is important to them, they usually do so. It's important to remember that you are seeking the customer's perception of the quality of your service.

Whatever approach you choose, preparation is the key. Start with your marketing department, if you have one, to examine any previous surveys or studies that might give clues to issues of importance. You may also want to interview certain managers or employees to discover any concerns they have about customers' perceptions. From this information you develop several guide questions to take into the interviews. Figure 7-2 shows a protocol for a generic focus group interview.

CONDUCTING THE FOCUS GROUP INTERVIEWS

One of the critical decisions that needs to be made is how to capture and preserve the qualitative data you get from your focus groups. At a minimum, consider audiotaping them. Careful note taking is important, however, the audiotape assures that you have a basis for checking your recorded comments. Even better, give serious consideration to videotaping the interviews.

You want to capture all the information that is volunteered as accurately as possible and that makes a big argument in

FIGURE 7–2

XYZ Corporation

Focus Group Protocol

Group Identification:_____

Date: _____ Start   Time: _____ End   Time: _____

Interviewer(s): _____

Interviewer: Hello, everyone. This is my colleague, Mary. Thank you all very much for making time to be with us today. Our discussion will be informal, so feel free to relax and ask any questions or make any comments you'd like. I'd like to start by asking some general questions about XYZ.

Guide Questions:

1. When you think of XYZ Corporation, what comes to mind?

2. In general, what is it like to be a customer of XYZ?

3. As customers of XYZ, what is your perception of the overall quality of service.

4. Have you ever had any problems as a customer?

5. What do you like best about XYZ stores?

Interviewer: Now I'd like to ask some questions about our products:

Questions about XYZ specific products.

Interviewer: I'd like to focus now specifically on the customer service aspects of XYZ.

Questions about specific aspects of customer service.

Interviewer: Let me follow up on some of the points you raised ...
(the interviewer probes further as comments are received from the focus group.)

Interviewer: If you had all the store managers and employees here right now, what would you like to say to them?

Interviewer: We want to thank all of you again. Here's an envelope for each of you and you'll find your honorarium inside.

favor of using video recording. However, some participants may clam up when they realize they're on T.V. This is less of a problem now than it was a few years ago. The wide proliferation of home camcorders has served to diminish a good deal of self-consciousness about video recording.

We have found that while interviewees are somewhat self-conscious at first, a skilled interviewer helps them quickly forget about the camera and get into the meat of the interview. Also, having the equipment set up and ready to go, so that the volunteers can look it over, peer through the camera viewfinder, and see themselves on the television monitor before the session, lessens the fear about being videotaped. Universities often videotape participants in interviews from behind one-way glass, with the participants' knowledge. We advise against it in a business setting. Too much of a "Big Brother" image.

If you do decide to videotape your focus groups, be sure to tell your prospective participants in advance, preferably in the recruiting letter. Tell them their identities will not be revealed by name, and that the videotapes will be used for research purposes only. You will need to get a release signed by each of them if you wish to use any segments of the videotape to show to others. A release form can be as simple as Figure 7–3 below. In addition to providing an accurate record of the focus groups, excerpts from these videotapes can be edited into a powerful 20 to 30 minute message for management and employees to see. We've used these edited excerpts to show company execu-

FIGURE 7–3

Release Form

I understand that the focus group in which I am participating is being audio/videotaped. I give my permission to XYZ Industries to show my image and use my voice for internal use only. I understand that I will not be identified by name and that this videotape will not be shown outside XYZ Industries in any public setting.

Signed _____ Date _____

tives what a small sample of their customers have to say, and it usually creates what we call an "interocular impact," that is, it hits them between the eyes. A similar effect is gained when the segments are shown to employees during orientation or training sessions. The immediacy of the video and the realization, "These are my customers talking to me," helps make the service advantage message come alive. If you're using focus groups for an internal climate assessment of your organization, you should not use videotape. Employees might not speak as freely if they know their remarks may be seen and heard by top management.

Response Biases

When interviewing people you can expect their responses to be biased by their individual frames of reference. That is why it is unwise to generalize to all of your customers based upon results obtained from a few focus groups. Even carefully designed surveys and questionnaires are subject to response biases.

Because of response bias it is important to allow answers given to your questions to be phrased by respondents in ways that make sense to them. The interviewer should record, as verbatim as possible, the statements and comments made by members of the focus group. That is another reason we suggest two interviewers. While one asks questions, the other records answers. After the focus group discussion is completed, the two interviewers can compare perspectives on what the participants said. Videotapes can be viewed and replayed to check these perceptions.

Questioning Techniques

One of the ways of managing response bias is through the use of careful questioning techniques. What will you ask your volunteer focus group participants? And how? You want to elicit their honest impressions of what it's like to do business with you. There are three types of questions that are used most frequently in interview research: *open-end, probe,* and *closed-end.* Here, for example, is an open-end question: "What has been your experience when you come to XYZ stores to buy something?" Another: "What do you like or dislike when you come here?" Stated this way, the questions cannot be answered with a simple yes or no.

The *probe question* is a follow-up inquiry based upon an answer or comment that someone has just given. Suppose you had just asked your group, "What do you think of our Product X?" and one of the participants replied, "I think Product X is hard to use." You need to find out what the customer means by hard to use. So you ask a probe question: "You said there were some problems in using Product X. Could you tell me a bit more about that?"

A third kind of question that you will use, but much less frequently than open-end or probe questions, is the *closed-end question.* Closed-end questions produce factual responses but don't provide much insight. A closed-end question might be, "How many times did you visit our store on 32nd street in the past year?" Another example: "Do you shop here often?" You'll find that you use closed-end questions more frequently when you're compiling factual or demographic data.

You can see that your abilities to listen carefully to the respondents, manage the group dynamics, watch your time constraints, and make sure that everyone in the focus group gets to speak, is a tall order. That is why so many companies prefer to leave focus groups to professional interviewers and researchers.

Staying Tuned In

As the focus group participants respond to your questions and react to one another's comments, your task is to be sure you understand clearly what they are saying. The interviewer must use excellent listening skills to get at the heart of the customer's perceptions. This also helps make the case for having a co-interviewer to take careful notes. Here are some suggestions to help you stay tuned in to your customers during the focus group session:

1. *Listen Actively.* When you listen actively you pay attention not only to what your customer says, but to how she or he says it and looks like when saying it. The tone of voice, posture, and facial expressions are all valuable clues as to what's going on inside the person's head. These are the clues that will help you know when to use probe questions to develop more detail. You have to maintain eye contact and focus on the content of the respondent's comment or answer.

2. *Clarify.* If you don't understand the customer's response, you won't be able to extract much useful data from it. Simply say, "I'm sorry, I don't quite follow you. Could you state that again?" or, "Would you help me understand what you just said a little better?"

3. *Paraphrase.* Your ability to rephrase another person's words in such a way that the respondent is satisfied that you truly understand them is critical. You might say, "Let me be sure I understand. You're saying you prefer to have our salesperson explain the credit policy verbally rather than handing you the information to read, is that correct?"

INTERPRETING THE RESULTS

The value of focus group interviews is that they allow you to spot *emergent themes* that represent concerns customers have about your business product or service. An emergent theme is a topic or subject that is mentioned by several persons in different focus groups. When the same notion is expressed by seven or eight different focus group participants without any suggestion or probing on the interviewer's part, you can be certain you have an emergent theme. There could be many emergent themes. With one client, we found more than 80 themes emerged during the focus group interviews.

The emergent themes provide you with guidance to the construction of surveys and questionnaires. You will want to find out if these themes that were expressed by numerous people in the focus groups hold true for a representative sample of your customers. That's when you will begin to make use of quantitative methods to verify your focus group data. More about that later.

Attribute Analysis

When the focus group interviews are completed, you will probably have several hours of videotape recordings, as well as a good-sized pile of interview notes. Making sense of all of the data is the next step. During the interviews you will have made notes about recurrent themes that were mentioned by the various focus group participants. These themes need to be placed into categories. They can also be ranked by frequency of response (how many times they were mentioned), or by intensity (the apparent strength of feeling when participants expressed them).

There may be many emergent themes, but there are probably only a few that could be termed "key attributes." These are the points that appear on your customers' mental report cards and upon which your business is judged as to the quality of service. Following, in Figure 7–4, for example, is a list of critical factors that could have emerged from focus groups with fast-food restaurant customers:

FIGURE 7–4

Key Attributes

1. Convenient location of the restaurant.
2. Fast and courteous service at the drive-up window.
3. Clean environment, outside and inside.
4. Fast and courteous service at the inside counter.
5. High quality food, properly cooked.
6. Attractive packaging and presentation of the meal.
7. Convenient operating hours.

While the fast-food restaurant owner might suspect, or even know from past experience, that the attributes listed above are desirable to his or her customers, the focus groups allow these factors to emerge from the customers themselves, thus adding to their potency. To verify the desirability of each attribute and to assess how the restaurant is doing in each category, a formal survey or questionnaire could be devised. Questions would be developed for each of the seven key attributes, and a representative sample of the restaurant's customers would be surveyed. The results of the survey data will confirm critical moments of truth that must be managed if the restaurant hopes to score high on the customers' report cards.

Domino's, the pizza chain, invites customers to be members of a "customer advisory board." Phil Bressler, regional director for the chain, brings in 8 to 10 customers from the advisory board every 10 weeks to talk about the quality and delivery of pizza. The group is called back 10 weeks later to see if service has improved. The 18 stores Bressler oversees have the lowest percentage of nonreturning customers (1.8 percent) among 3,800 Domino's outlets.[5]

CASE: ACCOR

Skillful customer research enabled Accor, a French hotel and catering service company, to launch a highly successful low-priced budget motel product very quickly. According to cochairman Paul Dubrule:

> We thought we perceived a possibility for an ultra-low-price motel product, located along motorways and near airports and train lines. But we weren't sure. So we launched an investigation into the perceptions of budget-oriented travelers. They told us they would be happy with a room for 100 francs (about $20 American at the time); it could have a simple but comfortable bed, a telephone, and a small closet. It did not have to have its own shower or toilet. We could have one such facility for each four rooms. We built a pilot version in a very short time, and it was booked full within a few weeks after it opened. Now we're building many more of them.

The Formula 1 motel chain, as it is called, is sort of the ultimate in a stripped-down accommodation. It can be operated by one couple, who only hire maid services when it is completely full. It offers a very simple check-in and check-out process, no porters, and no eating facilities other than vending machines. Formula 1 motels are often located very close to Accor fast-food restaurants or steak houses, to capture synergy sales. What is important to note in this case is that the *key attributes* discovered by talking to travelers—simple but comfortable bed, telephone, small closet, not necessarily a private bath or shower—confirmed Accor's hunch about this profitable new venture. If they had not conducted the interviews, they might have spent thousands of dollars on private shower and toilet facilities which the budget-minded travelers were willing to use on a shared basis.

CASE: SANTA MONICA HOSPITAL

We conducted a full service management implementation at Santa Monica Hospital in Santa Monica, California. To the best of our knowledge, Santa Monica was the first hospital in the United States to implement service management throughout the institution. Other hospitals have since initiated service management programs, including Poudre Valley Hospital in Fort Collins, Colorado; Santa Clara Medical Center in Santa Clara, California; and San Bernardino Community Hospital in San Bernardino, California.

We began the project at Santa Monica by examining existing marketing information the hospital had obtained in previous years concerning patient attitudes about service. It was decided to conduct new research to identify key attributes held by patients, employees, and physicians.

We conducted three focus groups with patients. A local research firm arranged for the volunteers, which included patients who had been hospitalized at Santa Monica within the previous two years, some who had never been hospitalized there, and some patients who had been admitted prior to the two year period. The focus groups contained 12 persons each. Two interviewers conducted each focus group, one asking questions and the other recording responses.

We found that some patients were exceptionally well-spoken and descriptive in the focus groups. We invited them to participate in a third focus group, which was videotaped with the patients' permission. We obtained release forms from them, agreeing to let the hospital use the videotapes as part of a service management training session.

In-depth interviews were conducted with physicians who were on staff and who had admitting privileges at Santa Monica Hospital. We asked the physicians to score the hospital in a head-to-head comparison with one of the hospital's major competitors. Three macroissues and twelve key factors emerged and were later measured in a survey we conducted of 600 physicians (see Figure 7–5).

To preserve confidentiality, the actual scores on the data below are not included.

Finally, we examined data obtained from an internal climate survey that Santa Monica Hospital had conducted shortly before we began the service management implementation project. We decided to conduct focus groups with employees to see if there were any new internal issues that needed to be surveyed. Focus group interviews with four employee groups did not indicate any new key attributes, so we were able to use the existing data as a basis for making implementation project plans.

When all the interview research was finished, we had accumulated very valuable data for our client. Using the results from customer focus groups of the hospital's quality of service, the physicians' assessments, and the employee climate data, the executive team mapped out a strategy to guide the hospital's future development.

Summary

Interview research is the most frequently used tool to begin to create key attributes that appear on your customer's report cards. One-on-one, in-depth interviews, and focus groups are the most commonly employed techniques. Interview research yields rich qualitative data about customer perceptions. And

FIGURE 7–5

**Santa Monica Hospital Medical Center
Research Model—Physician Expectations**

1. *Service to the physician in his or her work*
    a. Facilities available to the physician
    b. Equipment available to the physician
    c. Nursing support available to the physician
    d. Support services available to the physician (labs, etc.)

2. *Service to the physician's patient*
    a. Atmosphere of the hospital
    b. Attentiveness of nurses and support people to the patient
    c. Compliance with physician's instructions for patient care
    d. Personal services given to the patient

3. *Treatment of the physician as a business partner*
    a. Marketing and PR by the hospital to enhance business
    b. Listening to the needs and concerns of the physician
    c. Inviting physician to participate in hospital direction
    d. Sense of belonging, *esprit de corps* toward medical staff

don't forget to include internal customers, the people who work in your organization. Individual interviews and focus group discussion sessions will allow the key attributes to emerge. These attributes become the building blocks for the next step in getting to know your customer: conducting statistically valid survey research.

NOTES

1. Patricia Sellers, "Getting Customers To Love You," *Fortune,* March 13, 1989, p. 40.
2. Ibid.
3. "A kinder, gentler IRS? '88 forms were given full consumer testing," *The Denver Post,* January 1, 1989.
4. Sellers, *Fortune.*
5. John Hillkerk, "Domino's Service No Game", *USA Today,* July 21, 1987, p. 7.

CHAPTER 8

SURVEYS: WHEN, WHY, AND HOW

So, you've decided to "take a survey." You want to ask some questions of your customers because you need information. You've concluded that conducting a survey will help you make marketing decisions or make changes in your operation that will improve the service you give to your customers.

If you are a novice at surveying, you may think it is a simple matter to just "make up a questionnaire and send it out." That approach will give you an excellent opportunity to learn the hard way. You will be amazed at how many ways there are to do it wrong, and you'll probably have a chance to experience all of them if you take the trial and error method.

If you have carried out survey projects before, you know there are certain pitfalls to avoid, and certain things to keep in mind that will help you save time, resources, and energy. Planning and preparation pay off. If you carefully think through your entire project at the start, before you write a single question, you will greatly increase your chances of getting useful information with a minimum of work and frustration.

There are five phases to a successful survey project:

1. Planning your survey project.
2. Creating your questionnaire.
3. Collecting your data.
4. Processing your data.
5. Reporting your results.

Let's take a closer look at each phase.[1]

PLANNING THE SURVEY PROJECT

The first step in planning your survey project is to *specify your business objective*. What are you trying to accomplish? How would a survey help you accomplish that objective? The more precisely you can state your business objective, the more clearly you will be able to define the information you need and what you have to do to get it. Typical objectives that might lead to a customer survey include: deciding whether or not to offer a certain new product or service, getting more people to buy your current product or service, deciding how to improve or redesign your products, identifying a competitor's weak spot, or identifying newly emerging customer preferences.

In each of these cases, if you know what business objective you want to achieve, you can define your survey objective clearly. Your survey objective is what you want the survey project itself to accomplish.

For instance, if your business objective is to increase word of mouth referrals for your service, your survey objective will probably be to find out what factors cause customers to make referrals. To find that out, you will need to define the factors you want to measure. Only then can you compose a questionnaire that offers any hope of getting the right information.

As another example, your overall objective might be to get certain types of people to try your product. In this case, your survey objective might be to identify the factors that prevent people from trying it. Or you might want to find out why those who have tried the product decided to try it. You might want to go after both types of information.

Good customer information can often have a big impact on your business decisions. A university extension in California conducted a survey of its adult students, who were enrolled in a certain business program. Out of 950 surveys mailed to the students, over 400 came back from the postal service as undeliverable. Not only were those students no longer actively involved in the program, but the extension no longer even knew how to contact them. Of the 300 usable responses, only about 60 percent reported themselves as actively pursuing their programs. A number of students commented that the university no longer offered certain courses they needed to complete their programs, so they simply dropped out. This new information about the customers forced the planners at the extension to completely redesign their program and to undertake a brand new promotional effort to get the students involved and active again. Without the survey, they would have simply coasted blissfully along assuming that they had over 900 students, when in fact they had less than 200.

Good survey data can provide the basis for business decisions that may affect the success and even the survival of your business.

State Bank of South Australia, located in Adelaide, discovered the importance of good customer data in formulating its service strategy. Chief Marketing Manager Ron Dent says, "We've done a great deal of market research over the years, but we've never really made good use of the information. We knew a number of things about our customers, but we hadn't had a framework for analyzing it and drawing business conclusions from it. We asked Karl Albrecht to come to Australia and work with us extracting strategic meaning from our customer data. As a result of what we learned, we have significantly reoriented our concept of the business, its customer interface, our competitive strategy, and our internal service processes."

The design of your survey questionnaire, in terms of the number of questions, the content of the questions, and the way you present the questions, should follow logically from your survey objective.

Another consideration in setting your objective is the eventual reader of the report. Who wants the information? If you are the only "consumer" of the survey information, then you have a great deal of flexibility in the way you arrange the final results. On the other hand, if the reader will be a very busy executive, who has little time for plowing through numbers, you will need to think carefully about how to simplify the final results and present them in "consumable" form.

Before you jump into the process of writing up a questionnaire, consider all of these factors carefully. If you know exactly what you want to accomplish, your questionnaire will be as short and simple as possible, your data processing task will be as easy as possible, and the impact of your survey report will be as strong as possible.

Whom Should You Survey?

Once you have a clear objective in mind, the next step is to identify your target population. Who has the opinions you want to measure? This is an important decision to start with, because if you don't choose the proper target population you could waste time and effort gathering irrelevant data.

Many times the target population will be obvious. A doctor might want to survey his or her customers to see how they feel about the medical care and services they receive. Or, the doctor might want to know how they feel about the care they receive from the staff at the hospital.

A restaurant manager might want to ask the customers how they like certain menu items. The owner of an office supply store might want to find out how big the store's customer territory is by finding out how far away the customers travel to shop there.

In these cases, it makes sense to conduct a survey among the basic population at hand. But in certain situations, you may have to choose your population carefully. For example, a political campaign manager might want to measure the attitudes of people toward the candidate. It is too expensive to survey each of the people in a city of several million. So a representative sample of the overall voter population is selected. Herein lies the risk of error.

For example, the city may have a number of neighborhoods that differ widely in ethnic make-up, sociocultural level, income, and education. The fact that fewer people vote at the lower sociocultural levels could distort the picture if those people are the only ones in the sample population.

Similarly, it would not make sense to survey only the residents of a senior citizens' retirement village, looking for information about products for sports and fitness. To find out how people feel about experiences in hospitals, it would not be a good idea to survey only people who have never been hospitalized.

The examples cited above may seem obvious, but there are many cases in which the choice of a sample population can have hidden pitfalls not obvious to the survey taker. There is a famous story about the presidential campaign between Franklin Roosevelt and Alf Landon in 1936. The *Literary Digest* conducted a large opinion poll, which showed Landon the likely winner. However, in the election Roosevelt won by a healthy margin.

The *Digest's* pollsters had selected a large number of names from the telephone directories of major cities around the country. This produced a highly "skewed" sample, which included only city dwellers with incomes high enough to afford telephones. It eliminated virtually all investigation of the rural population, most of whom apparently favored Roosevelt.

As you decide on your sample population, look closely at the factors you want to explore. If you have used focus groups to help generate these factors, so much the better. Make sure the people you plan to survey really represent the overall population you are interested in, and that the conclusions you draw from the survey population will be valid for the rest.

On the other hand, don't think you must survey every single person in the overall population just to avoid sampling biases. By choosing your respondents carefully, you can usually make sure you will get information about each of the major subpopulations involved. If you are trying to find out the views of a customer population of 10,000 people, it really isn't necessary to survey all 10,000. Probably 1,000 good samples, or even less, if properly chosen, will give you the same results as if you had surveyed the entire group.

Even the famous Gallup poll-taking organization often uses only about 1,500 samples to find out the views of Americans on certain current issues, even though the adult population is well over 100 million. It is not so much a matter of surveying the right number of people as it is surveying the right people.

Define Your Research Model

If you want to design a good customer survey questionnaire, don't just sit down and start writing questions. This is the most common way to do it, but it is also the least effective. If you don't have an organized approach to defining the information you want, your questionnaire will probably end up a hodge-podge of vague, redundant, overlapping, or confusing questions with no common theme, and you'll probably have far too many questions.

Expert survey designers typically start by defining a "research model"—a list of critical information factors they want to explore. A research model gives you a logical basis for deciding what questions to ask. This is where the focus group research really pays off. If you've done the focus groups you can be more confident that the questions you're asking in your survey are the ones that your customers are truly concerned about. The research model also serves as a useful basis for discussing the survey project with others who may be involved.

Instead of starting with a list of questions, start with a list of topics about which you plan to write questions. Check this list against the list of factors you discovered in your focus groups interviews. This will save you a great deal of unnecessary revising, debate, and false starts.

As you work out your research model, ask yourself whether you will want to repeat this survey in the future. If you do, then you will want to be extra careful to define the research model so that it includes the kind of variables you want to observe over the long term.

CREATING YOUR QUESTIONNAIRE

Let's assume that so far you have analyzed your focus group data and have identified several themes that need to be validated with a survey. For each theme or factor in your research model, list one or more questions you will need to ask in order to investigate that factor fully. Don't bother about the exact phrasing of the questions at this point; just decide on the gist of the question. You may find that one factor requires several questions, while another might require only a single question. This is a matter for judgment on your part.

As you begin thinking about the overall design of your questionnaire, keep in mind that you will need to gather both demographic information and psychographic information. You need to have questions for both kinds of information.

Demographic information, you will recall, deals with general human characteristics that serve to identify specific segments of the population. These include such factors as age, gender, occupation, education, marital status, family income, religion, and zip or postal codes. This kind of information gives you a statistical overview of your sample population.

Psychographic information deals with opinions, attitudes, beliefs, preferences, value systems, social habits, and expectations. The opinion factors in your research provide the psychographic information you will need.

Make a list of the demographic and psychographic factors that are necessary for your survey project. These factors will become an important part of your research model.

Again, the factors you choose will depend on your judgment about your needs for information. Don't cram a long list of demographic questions into your survey just to be safe. Keep the questionnaire as short as possible. But do make sure you measure those demographic variables that will be important to you when you interpret the survey results.

Consider putting your demographic factors at the end of your survey. That way they won't distract your respondents, and they can answer the psychographic questions while their minds are still fresh.

Decide whether to make the questionnaire anonymous, or to have the respondents identify themselves. It is customary to make surveys anonymous when the answers to the questions involved might somehow single out the respondents and make them feel apprehensive about being subjected to recrimination, reprisal, or sales pitches.

In the rare instance when the identities of the respondents are important to your results, make sure the questions are nonthreatening, or you will probably get very few responses. When in doubt, make it anonymous.

Next, decide whether you want to subgroup the respondents in any way when you process the data, and if so, how. For example, you might want to subdivide the respondents by gender, age, or income level. You might want to subdivide them into buyers and nonbuyers of your product. If you do, you must include questions on your questionnaire that capture those factors.

You might choose to physically sort the questionnaire responses into the appropriate categories when they come in. In this case you might simply choose to put an extra item somewhere on the answer sheet that the person can fill in to identify his or her category.

Here are some other factors to consider as you design your survey questionnaire. The most effective surveys are the ones that are:

1. Easy to present to the respondent.
2. Easy for the respondent to fill out.
3. Easy for you to process.

In order to be effective, a survey must not be too long. People don't like to get bogged down with surveys that ask many questions and take a long time to fill out. A good rule of thumb is that if your survey is longer than 50 questions or so, your results will become increasingly less trustworthy. This is because, as people take the survey, their level of concentration begins to deteriorate after a long period of answering questions. They may start out feeling helpful and cooperative, but they can start to feel irritated and resentful as the survey drags on with item after item.

Not only will a very long questionnaire be more tedious for your respondents to fill out, but it will take much more effort on your part to process the data. It will also take a great deal of effort to explain the data to the people who will need to know the results.

Many poorly designed surveys are redundant; they ask for the same information in different questions. The most practical length for a survey is about 25 to 30 questions, or even less if possible.

Even though you now have a general approach to the design of your questionnaire, you are still not ready to start writing the actual questions. There are several more factors you need to consider that can affect the design. The important thing is to carefully analyze and organize your investigation, so as to come up with the most effective results.

Decide on the Size of Your Survey Population

The next step in planning your survey is to decide how many samples you will need to make your survey effective and worthwhile. You will need to choose a large enough sample to be confident in the results. On the other hand, you don't need an unnecessarily huge sample. Depending on your needs and the size of the survey, anywhere from 100 to 1,000 respondents may be enough of a population. One rule of thumb is to choose a data base of at least 100 respondents, unless your total available sample population is smaller.

Keep in mind that your survey population must be larger than the respondent population you hope to get, because you will rarely, if ever, get a 100 percent response rate. In fact, you probably won't even come close. It is very typical for mail surveys to show response rates in the neighborhood of 20 to 30 percent. So you will have to mail out many more questionnaires than the number you want.

Calculate the number of questionnaires you will have to send out. You can determine this by dividing the number of responses you will need by the decimal value of the response percentage you expect to get. As an example, say that you expect a 20 percent response rate, and you need at least 100 responses. You must therefore send out at least 500 questionnaires. In other words, 20 percent of 500 questionnaires will give you 100 responses.

Be aware of response biases. Some people will be more likely to return the survey if they are angry about some factor in the survey. Those who are more content may be less likely to complain, via the survey. Certain categories of people may respond more than others because of special interests.

Expect a certain number of unusable replies; 5 to 10 percent is not unusual. Some people may misunderstand the questions or the instructions, and may give responses that don't make sense. No matter how clearly worded your questions and your instructions, there will still be some people who are fuzzy in their thinking processes and can't fill it out. Other people may use the survey as a forum for their sarcasm, anger, or wit, and thereby invalidate their responses. A few people may choose to make nuisances of themselves by giving frivolous or nonsensical answers. You will need to make an extra allowance in planning the size of your survey population, to offset the effect of these unusable replies.

If you are concerned about getting a high enough response rate, you can use certain techniques to increase the percentage. One is to make sure the envelope in which you mail the questionnaire is attractive and looks like a piece of correspondence rather than a mass-mailed piece.

Another response technique is to put a "teaser" message on the outside of the envelope, offering some small gift which you explain inside. This gets more people to open the envelope, and once they have opened it they are more likely to fill out the questionnaire.

A well-proven response-building technique is to include money with your questionnaire. You can insert a dollar bill, or the equivalent if you are in a country other than America, as a token. Explain in your cover letter that you really need the respondent's opinion. This technique typically brings a response rate two or three times as high as the standard method. Apparently, many people cannot bear to pocket the money without helping out the survey taker.

How to Design Your Questions

When you have a clear idea of what you want to find out with your survey project, have defined a logical research model for your questionnaire topics, and have carefully planned the project, you are ready to create your questionnaire.

Study your research model carefully, making sure it will meet your needs. The questions you create must be brief and concise enough to get the point across using a minimum of words.

If you are working with a group or task force, don't let a committee write the questions. Have one literate person compose a draft and let others comment. Know when to stop nit-picking and get on with it. Get agreement on the objective of each question, but not necessarily on the exact wording.

It is very important to phrase your questions skillfully to make sure you get reliable answers. If your respondents misunderstand your questions, you will misunderstand their answers. Here are some guidelines to keep in mind as you compose your survey questions.

1. Keep each question as short as possible.
2. Use simple, concrete terminology. Avoid terms the reader might not know. You'll be amazed at the number of ways people can misread or misinterpret questions.
3. Ask only one thing with each question. Avoid "compound" questions, such as: "How do you like the quality and selection of our merchandise?" The customer may think your quality is high but your selection is poor, or vice versa; he or she won't know how to respond to the question. In some cases, you may want to combine two factors, but be careful not to combine disparate factors that will confuse the respondent.
4. Use a simple and consistent pattern of presentation in the wording of your questions.
5. Use "you" when possible; make it personal. You want the respondent to answer from his or her own point of view.
6. Avoid "loaded" questions that suggest that certain positive or negative evaluations are appropriate. In other words, don't "shop" for answers.
7. Minimize mental gymnastics in answering the questions; don't make the respondent do calculations or work out logical conclusions.

There are three common choices in phrasing questions: You can use multiple-choice questions, numeric questions, or comment questions. Use a multiple-choice question when you can offer the person a list of preestablished answers that will tell you what you want to know, for example, male/female, education levels, or degrees of product satisfaction.

Use numeric questions for continuous variables like age, number of years at current residence, or the number of people in the family.

Use comment questions when there is no way to predict the nature of the answer. Comment answers allow the person responding to express the answer in his or her own words. Bear in mind that you will have to hand process comment-type questions. Use them sparingly. Usually, one open-ended comment question placed at the end of the survey will be adequate to pick up additional factors.

For most opinion surveys, it is customary to use multiple-choice questions as the primary means for asking people about their opinions. The multiple-choice form is familiar, easy to read, easy to answer, and easy to analyze.

For some question items, you might have trouble choosing between a multiple-choice or a numeric format for the question. With the question of age, for example, you can either ask for a specific number, or you can divide the range of expected ages into bands and assign each band to a multiple-choice option.

If you have any doubt about which format to use, think about how you will actually be using the information. Numeric questions allow you to make finer distinctions in the populations, because they are continuous variables. Multiple-choice formats, however, offer simplicity and convenience in processing the data.

Decide on the number of options for your multiple-choice questions. The most common scale for multiple-choice questions in opinion surveys is the five-point "Likert scale" type. Dr. Rensis Likert, of the University of Michigan, developed this scale many years ago for behavioral sciences research. It is widely accepted because it offers a convenient range of choices that meets the needs of most situations.

The Likert scale presents a person with five options, ranging from "least" to "most", or vice versa. There is some debate among the experts as to which sequence to present. Some people like to put the most "negative" or critical option first on the list and finish with the most positive option. Some people prefer to put the most positive option first and have the others progress "downhill."

Many survey takers like to make the multiple-choice question a declarative statement with which the respondent can agree or disagree using a scale from 1 through 5. An example is seen in Figure 8–1.

Whichever form you choose, use it consistently throughout your questionnaire. Don't change back and forth from using 1 as the highest and 5 as the lowest and then to 1 as the lowest and 5 as the highest. That will confuse your respondents, your data entry person, and probably yourself. It will certainly confuse the people who will read your survey report.

Also, keep the end user of the data in mind when selecting your multiple-choice scale. Most people are accustomed to associating high numerical ratings, such as 4 or 5, with positive evaluations. Using 1 for a high score and 5 for a low score can be confusing to them. When in doubt, stick to the old rule, "big number means good score."

From your research model that has your demographic and psychographic factors, write a question for each factor. Jot each question on a notecard. Gather the cards together and sort

FIGURE 8–1

Product X gives good value for the price.

    1 = Strongly disagree
    2 = Disagree
    3 = Neither agree nor disagree
    4 = Agree
    5 = Strongly agree

them into a logical sequence, so they flow from one topic to another. Ruthlessly eliminate every question that is not essential to the objective of your survey project. If you are using a computer-based system, such as *Custometrics,* you are now ready to begin entering the questions into your computer.[2]

How to Test Your Questionnaire

You now have a draft questionnaire ready for the "pilot" test, which is a dry run in which you ask a small number of people to fill out the questionnaire. The purpose of the pilot test is to discover any design flaws you might have overlooked.

Why is it so important to test your questionnaire? It quite often happens that all the question items seem crystal clear, logical, and consistent to the person who made up the questionnaire, and yet a pilot test will disclose that one or more of the questions can be misread, misunderstood, or interpreted in more than one way. The pilot test is your hedge against surprises that can occur so late in your project that you cannot go back and redo the survey. We strongly recommend that you pilot test your questionnaire if at all possible.

Contact a small number of people, say 10 or so, who would be willing to test your questionnaire for you. Make sure they are typical of the people who will be your target population. For example, if you want to survey hospital patients, ask people who have been hospitalized to test your questionnaire. If you want to survey people who are single, make sure your test group is single.

A cordial, meaningful cover letter is very important. When the respondent receives the survey form, he or she will read the cover letter first and decide instantly whether to fill out the survey or throw it away. The cover letter must appeal to the respondents' own motivations and their willingness to participate in the survey. Discuss the content of the cover letter as well as the research model with everyone involved in the survey project.

Assemble the draft version of the survey package, including the questionnaire, the answer sheet, and the cover letter.

Include also a feedback sheet on which you ask the people in the pilot test group to give you their comments and evaluations of the questionnaire. Ask them to give you answers to at least these questions:

1. Did the cover letter appeal to them and motivate them to fill out the questionnaire?
2. Did they understand the instructions?
3. How long did it take for them to fill it out?
4. Were any of the questions ambiguous, confusing, poorly worded, or hard to understand?
5. Did they understand the multiple choice options?
6. Do they have any specific suggestions for improving the questionnaire?

Make photocopies of the survey package. Deliver the copies of the survey package to your chosen pilot group and ask them to fill it out and return it. Use the same method of return that you plan to use with the actual survey.

Here's an alternative and simpler method for testing your questionnaire. Contact a small group of typical respondents directly. You can get about a dozen of them together for a meeting and ask them to fill out the questionnaire individually by following the instructions, with no coaching or explanations from you. After they have finished filling it out, ask them to give you their evaluations of the key questions specified above. Don't ask them to editorialize about the phrasing of any one question, but go through the questions one at a time and ask them for a show of hands telling you whether they understood each one.

Finalize Your Questionnaire

Combine all the best suggestions from your test group and make hand written corrections and notations on a single copy of the questionnaire. Using the marked-up version of the printed questionnaire as a guide, make the appropriate changes in the questionnaire.

Make a final review of your survey package before you reproduce it. Make sure it is attractive, logically arranged, easy to understand, easy to fill out, and easy to return. Here are a few final pointers to keep in mind about your survey package:

• Be careful of the layout of the pages if there are more than one. Some respondents may fail to turn the sheet over and may not realize they haven't filled out all the questions. You might want to call their attention to this point in your cover letter.

• Use thin paper in reproducing the questionnaire. You might be tempted to use a fancy paper stock to dress up the package, but consider that several hundred responses can make a very high stack. This can make it difficult for the data entry person to handle them, and eventually to store them for safekeeping.

• Urge the respondents to use the answer sheet instead of circling or writing their answers directly on the questionnaire itself. This will save your data entry person a tremendous amount of time by eliminating the need to turn the pages of every single questionnaire to find the answer values.

• If the answer sheet takes up two pages, have it photocopied "front to back" so it ends up on a single sheet of paper. Again, this can be an important factor in the time and effort required to enter the data.

Collecting Your Data

Once you have planned your survey project and created your questionnaire, you are ready to collect your data. This phase is fairly straightforward, but careful attention to detail will pay off. Here are the steps in collecting your data.

• Assemble your questionnaire package, which will include the following items:
Mailing envelope with postage and address label.
Cover letter.
Questionnaire.
Answer sheet.
Return envelope with address and postage.

• Photocopy or instant-print enough copies of your question-naire package to mail out to your survey population.
• Fold, stuff, seal, stamp, and mail your questionnaires.
• Receive and organize the responses.

A PRIMER ON SURVEY STATISTICS

This is a brief discussion of the essential statistics used in opin-ion surveys. It does not include the more advanced types of statistical procedures used by mathematicians and statisti-cians. It covers only the basics you need to know to do a suc-cessful survey project. If you are an experienced survey taker or someone highly trained in mathematics, you may want to skip the following discussion.

Measuring Opinions with Numbers

In order to analyze the opinions of groups of people, you must ask them questions in such a way that you can describe their answers numerically. There are two types of questions you can use to do this: the multiple-choice question and the numeric question.

With the multiple-choice question, you ask the respondents how they feel about a particular point or what demographic category they fall into, and you provide a list of predetermined options to choose from. By numbering these choices sequen-tially, you make it convenient for the respondents to circle or check off their choices. You also make it convenient for yourself to average the response numbers of many people to get a com-posite measure of opinion.

With a numeric question, you ask the respondent to supply a number that measures the factor you want to learn about. For example, you would often want to know the respondent's age, in order to average up the ages from all respondents and study subpopulations to see if age is an important factor in the kinds of opinions people have on a certain subject.

Of course, it's usually a good idea to invite the respondent to contribute any voluntary comments about the subject, so you will want to include at least one comment-type question on your questionnaire. However, only multiple-choice questions and numeric questions lend themselves to mathematical averaging. You must process comment questions "by hand," so to speak.

Calculating Averages

You are, no doubt, familiar with the process of calculating an average value for a numeric variable such as age. You simply add up all of the numbers for the respective ages of your respondents and then divide by the number of respondents. The result is the average age, or mean age.

However, the process for calculating the mean answer value for a multiple-choice question is a bit more involved, although still fairly simple. For multiple-choice questions you don't add up all of the answer values directly. Instead, you count up the numbers of people who chose each of the available options on the question and you use these frequency counts to calculate a weighted average, or mean.

As an example, for a 5-option multiple-choice question, you will have five frequency counts. That is, you will have the number of people who chose option 1, the number who chose option 2, the number who chose option 3, the number who chose option 4, and the number who chose option 5. These five subtotals will add up to the total population, or the total number of respondents. The procedure for calculating a weighted average is as follows:

You find the gross total by multiplying the number 1 by the number of people who chose option 1. Then multiply 2 by the number who chose option 2. Multiply 3 by those who chose option 3, and so on through option 5, or whatever number of options you have on your questionnaire.

You add up all these subtotals to get the gross total, and then you divide it by the total number of respondents. This will give you a weighted average, or a mean value, which is a number somewhere in the range of 1 to 5. This weighted average will often be a decimal value that lies between two adjacent numbers, such as 4.71. For a 10-point scale, this process will involve all 10 multiplications, and the weighted average will lie somewhere along the scale from 1 to 10.

Even though the multiple-choice question only has a fixed number of answers from which to choose, you can still use the weighted average as useful statistic. For example, if option 1 means the respondent is male and option 2 means she is female, then a weighted average of 1.5 on this question means that there are equal numbers of males and females responding. A weighted average, or mean value, of 1.22 would indicate a greater concentration of males, while a mean value of 1.89 would indicate a greater concentration of females.

Similarly, if you ask people to describe their job satisfaction on a 5-point multiple-choice scale where 1 represents very low satisfaction and 5 represents very high satisfaction, and the values 2, 3 and 4 represent degrees between the extremes, you might get a mean answer value of 4.08. This would indicate that most of the responses are clustered around the level of 4. By looking at the actual frequency values as well as the mean value, you can see how widely the answers are scattered among the options chosen by the respondents.

Presenting Survey Statistics

You can display the results of a series of questions conveniently by using a frequency table, which is a tabulation of all questions against all of the multiple-choice options. Each row of the table shows the frequency counts for one particular question. For a 5-point multiple choice scale, there would be five columns, each with the frequency count for the respective option, and there would be a sixth column showing the mean answer value, or weighted average. Numeric questions would not have numbers under the options columns, since they do not have options. They would show only the mean value in the final column.

You can also choose to rank the question items according to mean answer value. You simply arrange the items in order of increasing or decreasing mean value, so the reader can quickly spot the largest and smallest values.

For multiple-choice questions, you can choose to present the frequency counts in their basic form as raw numbers, or you can show them as percentages of the total population of respondents. Some people like to say, "Fifteen point three percent of the respondents rated our product as a 5." Others like to say, "Eighty-seven respondents rated our product as a 5." This is strictly a matter of personal preference.

Other Statistics

In addition to frequency counts and mean values, you can also have a useful statistic called the standard deviation. You don't need to know how to calculate a standard deviation because most survey software packages do the calculation for you. You only need to know what it means. The standard deviation of a group of answer values is a calculated number that tells you how "scattered" the readings are in relation to the mean value.

If the standard deviation is zero, you know that all of the answer values for the particular question item are identical. That is, there is no spread at all in the readings. If the standard deviation is large, say 30 or 40 percent of the mean value itself, you know that there is quite a bit of variation in the answer values.

It is also helpful to know the range of answer values for a question, that is, the lowest and highest values given. For multiple-choice questions you can spot the range just by glancing at the frequency counts. For numeric questions, most software will calculate the low and high values as part of the software's item analysis report.

Another sometimes useful statistic is the number of "no-response" cases. If a person simply doesn't supply an answer to a certain question, for whatever reason, you must not count that person as part of the population when you figure the average answer for that question. Your software program probably keeps a separate tally of no-response cases for each question. The total of the frequency counts for a question plus the no-response count will equal the total population of respondents.

That's basically all you need to know to work with questionnaire surveys. Most software programs do all of the figuring for you. All you have to do is get the data, enter it into your computer, and let your software do the rest.

PROCESSING YOUR DATA

As the replies come back, review each answer sheet carefully and discard the ones that are incomplete, suspicious, or otherwise unusable. Decide whether to subgroup the responses, or to enter them into a single composite data file on your computer disk. There are several factors to consider in making this decision.

Think ahead and consider the way in which you will be processing the data. If you will only want basic reports for various subgroups, and you won't be doing many studies of the whole respondent population, then you may want to physically sort the responses and enter them in separate groups. However, if you plan to study various characteristics of the whole population, and pull out reports for many different subpopulations, it may be better to have all of the responses together in a single data file.

For example, if you want to accumulate a report for all of the women in the survey population, and you have female respondents represented in 10 different regional data files, you will have to scan all 10 files to combine the results for all of the women. On the other hand, if you have a large population and you want to pull out many different subpopulations, you will find it tedious and time-consuming to wait while the computer scans through hundreds of responses on the data file, searching for only a few responses. You need a balance between these two extremes.

Organize the Response Sheets

Consider hole-punching the answer sheets and putting them into one or more large looseleaf binders for easy handling. This way, you can also store them for future reference if necessary.

Until you have finished processing the data and reporting the results, it is advisable to keep the answer sheets in a safe place against the possibility of a lost or damaged data disk, or a computer failure.

You will probably want to capture any handwritten comments the respondents have to offer by typing them into your word processor. Browse through the responses to see whether certain comments come up repeatedly. If so, ask the typist to simply list each of the comments and count the number of times each one occurred. The result will be a tabulation that is easy to read, showing the various comments and the number of occurrences of each. This narrative report will go together with your statistical reports to make up your complete survey report.

Begin by collecting all of your "big picture" reports for the subgroups chosen in one stack. Browse through each of them, to get an overall impression of the answer patterns. It's not possible, of course, to give an exact formula for this overview of the data, because the most noticeable answers will depend on your particular survey, and on your respondent population. There are, however, some general procedures you can use.

The first step is to perform an examination which some statisticians facetiously call the "interocular impact test." In other words, if any item on the report "hits you right between the eyes," in terms of an unusual or noticeable answer pattern, you probably need to follow up on that aspect of the survey. You might want to put a mark beside each of the question items that catches your eye.

For example, are the answer values to a certain question much higher or much lower than the answers to the other questions? Do any questions have a bimodal "split" pattern, that is, with many responses at the low end of the multiple-choice scale, many at the high end, but few in the middle? Do any of the questions have an unusual spread of answer values, with no apparent consensus?

Look at the demographic variables, to see what kind of people responded. What is the average age of your respondent population, and how does it compare with the overall survey population? Are males and females represented in your respon-

dent population in about the same proportion as the survey population, or might there be some bias that causes one sex to reply more numerously than the other?

Put a number of the big picture reports together as a group, overlaying them one on top of another, so that the mean value columns line up side by side. For each question item, compare the mean answer values across all of the subgroups, to see whether there are significant differences between subgroups on certain questions.

Look for significant differences in mean values. Small differences do not tell much of a story in most cases. For example, on a 1 to 5 Likert multiple choice scale, two mean values of 3.18 and 3.22 are probably not sufficiently different to invite special attention. However, two mean values like 2.83 and 3.35 may suggest a relatively important difference. Two values like 3.11 and 4.3 would certainly suggest a strong difference in the reactions of your respondents.

Contrasts often offer clues to where the action is in survey results. For example, if most of the mean values are running in the neighborhood of 3.2 on a 5-point scale, and you see a value such as 1.9, this particular factor may be especially significant to the respondents. Similarly, a mean value of 4.6 in this case would also be an attention-getter.

If you are working with a team or a task force, make some notes about your findings, reproduce the big picture reports you have so far, and have a meeting to discuss your findings with other members of your survey team.

Study Special Subpopulations

Whether or not you decide to pull out subpopulations from the data, and if so, which ones you choose, will depend on your objectives for the survey project. Decide what you really need to know about your respondent population.

In certain situations, you might want to compare males and females as separate groups. Or, you might want to look at the results for people who are older or younger than the average age. Or, you might want to look at the results for people in certain occupations, if your questionnaire included that fac-

tor. Or, in a company survey you might want to pull out responses from people who have been employed with the
company longer than a certain period of time.

It is often useful to split the respondent population in
terms of a single variable such as age. For example, if the average age of your respondent population is 42.3, you might
want to pull out a subpopulation of people whose ages range
from 0 through 42.3, and another subpopulation whose ages
range from 42.3 through 100. This high-low technique gives
you a convenient way to find out whether age, for example, is a
factor that influences the other answer values. You can do the
same thing with any other numeric question.

Plan to look at a minimum number of subpopulations first.
Pulling out many subpopulations can be tedious and time con-
suming for you, and reading the reports can be burdensome to
the eventual reader of the information. You may find that the
reports from a few carefully chosen subpopulations will give
you a fairly complete picture of the situation. It is always
tempting to try to split hairs by pulling out more and more
narrowly defined subpopulations, but be sure to focus on the
primary factors involved. Don't get sidetracked with secondary
variables and obscure relationships that don't shed light on
your overall survey objective.

You may want to examine the details of the various question items for certain groups, or for the whole respondent population. Item analysis will give you a breakdown for each
individual question. With most survey software you will see
the mean answer value, multiple-choice frequence counts, standard deviation, and the no-response count for each item. For
numeric questions, you will also see the range of answer values, in terms of the lowest observed value and the highest observed value for the group you are studying.

REPORTING YOUR DATA

Think carefully about the best way to present your results to
your client or sponsor, that is the "consumer" of the results.
For this discussion we will refer to this person as your *client.*

The first rule is: don't make the mistake of overwhelming your client with raw data. You will probably need to "predigest" the data to some extent and put it into understandable form.

This is the point at which many survey projects go off the track. If you have spent several hours, or even days, going through the survey data, you have probably become very familiar with it. You know the questions by heart, and you know what the results indicate. However, your client probably does not know any of these things.

If you just dump a stack of computer printouts on your client's desk without any preliminary explanation of the project, you can expect to cause confusion, frustration, and very little understanding. Be willing to invest some time and energy into putting your survey results into readable form.

There are two useful ways to present your survey results, and you can use both if you like. The first way is to prepare a written report. The second is to present the information in the form of a briefing.

To prepare a written report, think carefully about the reader. Who is it? What does the reader know about the survey project? Did he or she personally commission the project, or was it your idea? Are the objectives clear to everyone who must read the report, or should you explain them?

When you are thinking about the reader, ask yourself how that person likes to learn things. Is he or she a numbers-oriented, detail-minded person, or more of a generalist? How analytical is the reader's approach to statistical information? Will this person be more comfortable if you boil the results down to the essentials, or is it better to present all the details and have them share in the process of interpreting the results? If you don't have the answers to these questions, you might want to contact your client and ask for preferences before you prepare your report.

Based on the needs of your client, make an outline for your report. Think over this outline carefully and make sure it will enable you to present your results most effectively. Here is a typical format for a survey report:

1. Introduction.
2. Methodology of the project (how you did it).
3. Highlights of the findings.
4. Selected subgroup reports.
5. Narrative comments (transcribed from answer sheets).
6. Interpretations of the results (if appropriate).
7. Appendix (especially useful but detailed information).

In the introduction, spell out in a few paragraphs the nature of the survey project. Don't go into detail; just let the reader know briefly what the report is all about. Explain the objective of the survey project in terms of what you were trying to find out. Why did you do the project? What did you hope to learn? Relate the survey objective to the overall objective or project that led to the need for a survey.

In the methodology section, briefly describe the overall approach to the project. Answer questions such as: What population did you decide to survey? Why did you choose that population? What research model did you use, that is, what information factors did you settle on? How many items did you have on your questionnaire? Did you pilot test your questionnaire, and if so, how? How many questionnaires did you distribute? How did you distribute them? How many replies did you get? What response percentage does this represent?

In the highlights section, describe briefly your overall impression of the findings, if this is appropriate for your reader. Don't go into detail here; just give an overall picture of the results, to get the reader oriented to what is coming.

In the data section, provide copies of the computer printouts you feel will be most interesting and informative to the reader. You may want to provide samples of subpopulation reports and rankings for certain scans, but it is usually not necessary or effective to dump all of the printouts into your report. Provide only what you think the reader will need to understand the results at his or her level of interest and concern.

In the narrative section, present the transcribed comments made by the respondents, to give the reader a sense of the reality "behind the numbers." This kind of attitudinal and anecdotal information can help a great deal in forming an accurate impression of the viewpoints of your respondent population.

In the interpretation section, you can explain in some depth the conclusions you have derived from the survey data—again, if appropriate to your dealings with your client. Bear in mind that just about any survey can have response biases—hidden distortions due to differences in the attitudes of those who responded and those who did not. In the case of a mail survey, there is not much you can do to prevent these effects. You only know the opinions of those who responded to the questionnaire, not those who failed to respond. Keep some of these factors in mind as you interpret the results. Always be a bit cautious about making hard-and-fast conclusions from survey data. Keep an open mind for alternative interpretations of the results.

In the appendix section, you can include various tables and graphs that will help your reader make sense of the results. This is where bar and pie graphs and other graphic illustrations can make your report come alive. Always look for alternative and creative ways to present your data.

You will probably use a word processing software package to prepare a complete report. You may also want to dress up your report by having it printed or using a professional-looking binder to hold the materials.

Before you make copies of your report for distribution to your readers, go over the final version very carefully. Make sure there are no errors or inconsistencies in the data. Eliminate all spelling errors, grammatical errors, and typographical errors.

It is especially important that your survey report be accurate in all respects. There are some peculiar psychological effects that come into play when people read statistical data. If they see spelling errors, or errors in numbering the items on a list, for example, they tend to become suspicious of the data in the report.

People who read computer-generated reports expect the computer to be perfect, and they unconsciously tend to expect the writer of the report to be perfect as well. If the reader spots an inaccurate figure, or a figure that doesn't check out logically with the other figures, he or she will tend to doubt the validity of the overall presentation. So make sure your final report is correct in all respects, even in minor details. When you have checked all the details and decided your report is ready to go, have it reproduced and bound suitable for reading by your client.

NOTES

1. Some of the content in this chapter is adapted from *Custometrics Customer Satisfaction Survey System* © 1988 Dr. Karl Albrecht (San Diego: Shamrock Press). Used by permission.
2. You will probably use some kind of software that is geared to survey data production and sorting. We recommend *Custometrics,* a complete software package for the generation and interpretation of survey data. This program is for IBM and IBM compatible computers. For more information contact Shamrock Press, 1277 Garnet Ave., San Diego, CA (619) 272-3880.

CHAPTER 9

CREATE YOUR CUSTOMER REPORT CARD

Let's assume for the moment that you're the owner of a small business and you've done everything we've suggested so far. Up to this point you've been collecting and sorting out data from your customers. You've conducted focus group interviews, perhaps some individual interviews as well. From the focus groups and the in-depth interviews, you've discovered a number of factors that seem to be of importance to your customers.

You've looked carefully at the data from your customer perception research. You've constructed a pilot questionnaire and tested it out on a small group of respondents. They've given you feedback about the questionnaire and you've made the necessary changes. Your final version of your survey has been mailed out and now the results are pouring back in.

Now it's time to translate the raw data from your survey to information you can use to create a customer-focused operation. The starting point is the creation of an *attribute matrix*.

CREATING THE ATTRIBUTE MATRIX

You'll recall that in Chapter 4 we introduced the concept of *key service attributes* that your customers use to evaluate the quality of your organization's product and service. These attributes are used by the customer during the moment of truth to give your business a "grade" on the customer's report card.

Let's say you've done your homework and gathered up a lot of data about your customers' perceptions of your business. And you've found that five attributes continue to poke their heads up out of the data pile. Those five attributes seem to be the ones of most importance to your customers, to be sure, but what happens when the customer compares your business with your competitor down the block on these five attributes? How do you stack up against the competition when these attributes are compared in the customer's mind? And which attributes are most important to your customers? That's where the attribute matrix can help you make some sound decisions about your business.

Consider this case: You own a restaurant. You have a salad bar which you believe distinguishes your restaurant from the one across the street. You've discovered that your customers place high importance on cleanliness in the salad bar area. If the restaurant's salad bar area is clean and so is the competition's, how do the two stack up when compared?

All things being equal, which they seldom are, if both restaurants have clean salad bars and if that key service attribute is important to the customer, then you have a standoff. There is no differentiation in the customer's mind between your salad bar and the competition's salad bar *on the key attribute of cleanliness.*

"But," you say, "my salad bar is not judged only on cleanliness. What about our great variety of vegetables, and how about the way we display the food?" And, of course, you are exactly right. You've just identified more key service attributes that need to be compared to determine their desirability in your customers' minds. How important to your customers is the display? What importance do they attach to the variety of greens and toppings? Failure to compare key service attributes to each other and with those your competitors offer may cause you to overlook or undervalue the attributes that contribute to market differentiation. At the same time, it's possible that you're putting a lot of time, energy, and money into something that your customers don't think is very important.

But just knowing which attributes are important to your customer doesn't give you the whole picture. Your customers constantly grade you on each factor on their mental report cards. But they do something else as well. In a semiconscious way, they rank each of the key service attributes according to their importance. This weight is called *valence* and it's a measure of the relative desirability of attributes in relation to each other. You may want to know how the key service attributes you offer stack up against one another from the customer's perspective.

To do this, you use a tool called *conjoint preference analysis*. It's much simpler than the name implies. You simply ask customers to rank an attribute against all the other attributes that your business offers.

Suppose our restaurant owner wanted to compare the key attribute of "attractive display" to other key product attributes related to the salad bar. When preparing to survey the customers, the owner would probably include a series of questions like those listed in Figure 9–1.

By counting the number of choices made for each option the restaurant owner can determine the valence, or desirability of "attractive display" when compared with all the other attributes of the salad bar.

FIGURE 9–1

In each pair below, please check one box that represents what is most important to you when you visit our salad bar.

1.		3.	
☐	Attractive display	☐	Attractive display
	or		**or**
☐	Lots of raw vegetables (broccoli, cucumbers, etc.)	☐	Large variety of greens (spinach, lettuce, etc.)

2.		4.	
☐	Attractive display	☐	Attractive display
	or		**or**
☐	Hot soups available	☐	Variety of breads (crackers, rolls, etc.)

Of course, to find out how you score on a given attribute when compared to the competition, you have to ask your customers to make a head-to-head comparison between your performance and your competitor's performance on each key service attribute. If you can get a sense of the important attributes on your customer report card, then you can ask your interview or survey respondents to compare you with other businesses that provide the same product or service that you do.

SAS International Hotels, a division of Jan Carlzon's SAS Group, uses some sophisticated methods and models for finding out what its travelling customers want and making use of the information in product design and competitive decision making. According to Christian Sinding, SAS vice president for the SAS Hotels division, "We consider competitive analysis an integral part of customer research. We aggressively interview customers of our principal competitor on a regular basis. We interview as many as 2,000 of them a year, searching for clues that might lead to a strong competitive advantage."

The Service Attribute Matrix

To sort out the key service quality attributes, you create a matrix that displays one key attribute, along with that attribute's importance to customers, and a comparison between your business and your competitor on that one attribute.

The figure below illustrates the relationship between the *importance* of a service attribute and the level of *performance* on the attribute, as graded on the customer's report card.

Let's examine the attribute matrix a bit more closely. There are two major criteria by which the quality of your product or service are judged: the importance of a given attribute from the customer's perspective, and your performance grade in meeting the customer's expectation about that attribute. Importance ranges from low to high and is at the left of the matrix. Performance also ranges from low to high. You could apply any measurement criteria to these two axes you wish. You might use a scale of 1 to 10, or perhaps use letter grades

FIGURE 9–2
Attribute Matrix

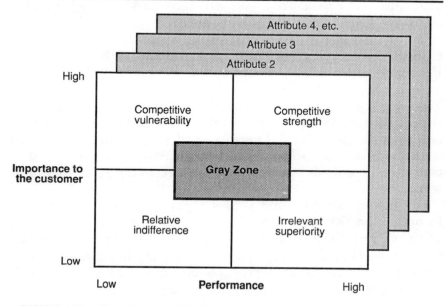

©1989 Karl Albrecht and Lawrence J. Bradford.

similar to an actual report card a youngster might receive. What is important is to assign some numerical equivalent to the performance axis.

The matrix has five zones where the importance of the attribute and your performance in delivering it intersect.

Competitive Vulnerability: High Importance/Low Performance

In this zone the attribute being assessed has high importance to the customer; however, if your grade on the customer's report card falls below the middle range, you have a low performance score. Where these two criteria—importance and performance—intersect is the Competitive Vulnerability Zone. In order to improve your competitive position on the particular attribute being measured, you will have to increase your performance level in the customer's eyes.

Competitive Strength: High Importance/High Performance

You hope most of your customers will rate your performance in this quadrant. To get there, you'll have to score above average or better in terms of delivering service. The attribute being measured has high importance to the customer, so you need to consistently deliver service at an above average or excellent level.

What if both you and your competitor score high on performance on this attribute? That's good news for you. It tells you that you're at least even or slightly better than the competition on this single attribute. What must happen next is to raise the performance scores on other attributes on which you've been rated lower than your competitors.

Relative Indifference: Low Importance/Low Performance

This is an unusual zone. It's the point at which importance of the attribute, in the customer's eyes, is relatively low. And your performance on the attribute is also relatively low—at the C level or lower. So this is a zone of relative indifference to your product or service.

It is also possible that the attribute being measured *should be* important to your customers, but, for some reason, isn't. Have you done an adequate job of educating your customer about the important aspects of this particular attribute? Does your customers' awareness of this attribute need to be elevated for their safety, comfort, or confidence?

What if your competitor seized this attribute and created a heightened awareness of its importance in the eyes of your customers, then demonstrated that he or she could outperform you? If that happened, you'd soon find yourself in a catch-up ball game.

Irrelevant Superiority: Low Importance/High Performance

This may be what Shakespeare had in mind when he penned, "Much ado about nothing." You may be spending a great deal of time, energy, and money in your business, striving to perform at a superior level on some attribute that *you* think is important to your customers, but that *they* really don't care about at all! Focusing too much on little, insignificant details that only marginally affect customer perception is a mistake. It's like trying to stomp on thousands of ants when there are elephants crashing through the ceiling.

On the other hand, if this is an attribute on which you can perform at high levels, perhaps you can raise your customer's perception about the importance of the attribute. If you can do that, you promote it from Irrelevant Superiority to Competitive Strength.

Gray Zone: Neutral Performance/Neutral Importance

Another name for the *Gray Zone* could be the *Zone of Indifference*. When the importance of the attribute being assessed is neither high nor low in the customer's perception, and when your performance score is somewhere in the middle range, you're probably in the Gray Zone. In this instance, your business is perceived as about average with everyone else who provides your product; neither better, nor worse. If that's the case, then you gain parity with your competitor, but you lose market differentiation. Your business is not distinguished from that of your competitors on the particular attribute being assessed in the matrix.

Continuing our restaurant example from before, suppose that "attractive display" is an attribute with high importance to customers. Data from your customer perception surveys indicate that on this attribute your customers graded you slightly below average. Your competitor, though, scored higher than you on the performance axis. Again, you must ask your customers to grade you head-to-head with your competition in order to get this information. Your performance on this attribute places you in the *Competitive Vulnerability* zone, while your competitor scores in the *Competitive Strength* zone. On this attribute of high importance to your customers, you are outscored by your competition.

It's important to remember that you must create a matrix for every one of the key service attributes which emerge from your research. If your business is like most others, you'll find there are a dozen or fewer key service attributes.

The attribute matrix is also useful if you're assessing your own organization's internal climate. You would change the "Importance to the customer" criterion on the left side of the matrix to "Importance to the employee." The attribute matrix is a useful way of checking the relative importance of your employee's perception about how well your company performs on a certain attribute.

State Bank of South Australia, located in Adelaide, discovered the importance of good customer data in formulating its service strategy. Managing Director Tim Marcus Clark identified service quality as the strategic thrust of his leadership at the bank. "If we're going to survive and thrive in the new Australian deregulated banking environment, we're going to have to become less focused on our navels and more focused on the customer," says Clark. "We've got to learn more about our customers' needs and interests and we've got to capitalize on what we learn."

State Bank discovered they were losing customers to their competitors at about the same rate, and for the same reasons, as they were getting customers from the competitors. Several critical moments of truth accounted for about 80 per cent of the transition events. Chief marketing manager Ron Dent says, "We're in a saturated market. It's become a zero-sum game; we get new customers mostly at the expense of other banks who lose them. We've got to focus much more keenly on managing the key moments of truth that tend to cause transitions."

PRIORITIZING THE ATTRIBUTES

Once you've created attribute matrixes for each of the key service attributes on your customer's report card, you'll need to decide what service target to shoot at first. This, of course, is a matter of your own judgment. However, we'd suggest you follow a procedure of ranking and rating the attributes so that you'll be sure to focus attention on the critical attributes first.

The conjoint preference analysis is one way to do it. Another is to rank order the attributes on the basis of their importance to your customers. You would simply ask your survey respondents to rank order the attributes according to their desirability. When you get the results you could assign an artificial number or weight to the importance scale, ranging, say, from 1 for the lowest importance up to 10 for the most important.

Then you can give each attribute a code name, color, or symbol. A handy way to look at all the attributes together is to take a piece of clear transparency film, such as that used for overhead projections, and draw the attribute matrix on it. Then write in the ratings for all the attributes on the transparency. By using different colors or symbols for each attribute, you can easily spot which of them is most important, and what your level of performance is for each one.

Still another way to capture all the data for prioritizing would be to create a line graph. One line would show the desirability rankings for all the attributes; the other would show the performance ratings. You could easily spot those attributes on which you were performing well or poorly and compare them to their importance, as perceived by your customers.

You could also prioritize the key service attributes by grade average. If you asked your survey participants to rate your service attributes with letter grades, it's a simple matter to figure out your "service point average." Just assign a number to each letter grade, then add up the total and divide by the number of responses you received. Using 1.00 as the lowest value and 5.00 as the highest, you'll get lots of averages with decimal points, such as 2.85 or 3.77. Again, don't be too concerned when ratings on various attributes are relatively close together, such as 3.25 and 3.30. Do pay attention to any on which there is a big spread between you and your competition, such as 2.20 for you and 3.50 for your competitor.

We lean more toward prioritizing attributes first on the basis of their perceived importance to the customer, then on the basis of performance ratings. If you want to be sure you focus on what's important to the customer, irrespective of how well or poorly you may be performing on a certain attribute; that's the best way to do it.

Let's assume that you've identified the service attributes which are most important or desirable to your customers. You still have to decide which of the many attributes that might emerge from your research are the ones upon which you should focus your service improvements. The task, then, is to pick those attributes that will constitute your *final service riteria.*

SELECTING THE FINAL SERVICE CRITERIA

Sooner or later you will have to make a decision. You'll have to choose, from the many key service attributes your customers have indicated, the ones that are most important and that you'll take on and make part of your final service criteria. They are the service attributes on which you will try to establish differentiation of your business from your competitors.

Here's an area where the small business has an inherent advantage over the big corporation. Because of its smaller size and less complex organizational structure, the small business can respond more quickly to change. If you're a small business owner you can change your product line or change internal policies much easier than a huge bureaucracy.

The taller and fatter an organization becomes, the more lumbering its gait when it comes time to begin movement toward some organizational change. Bureaucracies create networks that have more points at which approvals and disapprovals are given. Special interests intrude, and sometimes change is very slow to take place. But even dinosaurs need to move when danger or opportunity approach. The smaller organization can get up, move, and take advantage of windows of opportunity a good deal faster and easier than big operations.

You can use any criteria that makes sense to your business when you select the final key service attributes; however, be sure that you choose those your customers have rated as either of high or medium importance. Be sure you don't just discard those that were rated of low importance. There could be a gem of service there that only needs polishing to raise it to high visibility and high importance to your customers as you seek market differentiation.

So which of the service attributes in your attribute matrix will you choose to be your final service criteria? Let's try a hypothetical case. Suppose you own a real estate firm. You've conducted focus groups of various customers, you've also designed a questionnaire to establish the key attributes of importance to them, and the data you received from your survey shows that real estate customers consider 10 key attributes when they look for an agency to represent their property. The attributes, the importance of each, and the score you received on each attribute are seen in Figure 9–3.

These key service attributes could be prioritized on the basis of the grade given by the customer. In the hypothetical situation above, the second attribute would probably be a cause for concern since it is an attribute of high importance to your customers, and they perceive your performance level as C, which is only average or mediocre.

By contrast, attribute number eight is of low importance to the customer. It doesn't really matter to him or her if the agent drives by the property every day. The D grade indicates the customer also believes the agent doesn't do this very often.

To decide on your final service criteria, you should focus first on the service attributes your market research has shown to be of *high importance* to your customers. Next, you would weigh those of *medium importance*. The final consideration would be those attributes judged *low in importance*. Are there any of the four attributes judged low in importance that should actually be viewed with more importance by your customers?

Is it possible you could be spending too much time emphasizing the wrong behaviors on the part of your agents? For ex-

FIGURE 9–3

Attributes	Importance	Score
1. I trust the agent to represent my property honestly and ethically.	High	B
2. My agent is available when I call about my property.	High	C
3. The agent calls me frequently to keep me informed.	High	A
4. The agent dresses and acts professionally.	Medium	B
5. The agent shows my property to a great number of potential buyers.	Medium	C
6. The agent's "For Sale" sign is placed for high visibility.	Medium	A
7. The agent is warm and friendly to me.	Low	A
8. The agent drives by my property every day.	Low	D
9. The agent's office is attractive.	Low	B
10. The agent's office is located near my property.	Low	C

ample, attribute number seven, "The agent is warm and friendly toward me," is rated as superior—A—by customers. The agents are uniformly viewed as friendly, approachable, and warm. Yet, these attributes turned out to be of relatively little importance. Many businesses waste a sizable amount of money in what we call "smile training" because they don't assess the relative importance of attributes from the perspective of customers. As we see in the case above, if you focused an undue amount of training on programs to teach agents to be warm and friendly, you'd be making a poor business decision. On attribute number seven, our hypothetical agents are performing in the *Irrelevant Superiority* quadrant in the attribute matrix from Figure 9–2.

Bear with us on this case study a bit longer. Notice on the first attribute regarding honest and ethical representation of the property, customers generally viewed the company's performance at a B level—above average, but probably not superior to the competition. Attribute number two, having the real estate agent available when the customer calls about his or her property, is rated at a C level—about average. And the third attribute, concerning frequent calls by the agent to the property owner, is judged at an A—or superior performance level.

With this information, you can begin to make some reasoned judgments. Where would you start? The most important attribute is being performed reasonably well, but the second most important one is only average. The best performance is on the attribute of third-ranked importance.

In this hypothetical case it would make sense to choose the second ranked attribute as one of the final key service attributes, and to focus attention on raising that C grade performance to A work. Why is agent availability rated as only average by customers? Is there something wrong with your telephone system? Is the scheduling of agents' time being done efficiently? The solution could be to equip agents with cellular telephones so that they can be reached while they are out of the office or enroute from one property location to another.

The point we want to make here is that not all attributes have the same degree of importance to all of your customers. That's why it is imperative for you to segment your key service criteria by customer type and sample your customer opinion on a regular basis. That's the only way you can be certain that you're still focusing your service improvement efforts on things that are of importance to your customers. In other words, you must constantly *validate your customer's report card*.

VALIDATING THE REPORT CARD

One of the questions most frequently asked about customer perception research is, "How often should we do it?" Many owners of businesses, both large and small, are surprised when we tell them that last year's research may already be obsolete.

If your business is conducted in a competitive climate, as most are, you have to realize that your competition constantly looks for ways to gain a competitive edge, just as you do. You need to find out, on a regular basis, how you're doing in the eyes of your customers.

Have their tastes changed? Are the service criteria on which you base your treatment of your customers still valid? Has your competition introduced new or different products or services that could woo your customers away from you? Is everyone in your organization still "walking the talk" on service excellence? All of these are questions that can only be answered by validating your customer report card on a regular basis.

National Westminster Bank, headquartered in London, places a great deal of emphasis on knowing who their customers are demographically and understanding them psychographically. The bank uses a variety of questionnaires and interviewing techniques to pinpoint the habits and preferences of its branch customers. According to Paul Goodstadt, director of service quality, "We absolutely must keep our finger on the pulse of the customer. We want to know who our customers are, why they chose to bank with us, the details of their banking habits, and how they feel about every aspect of the interface we have with them. We need to know if we've messed someone around and we're about to lose that person as a customer. And we need to know what our real marketing opportunities are."

When you choose service excellence as a means of market differentiation you are not just "conducting programs." You are buying into a totally different way of running your business. That means that you'll have to constantly be sure that your performance on your customer report card is up to par.

To use a medical metaphor, think of your business as a patient. Your customer report card is a sort of bill of health, as viewed from your customer's perspectives. Just as a health-conscious person goes for regular check-ups, so should you submit your business to a kind of annual physical to check the state of its health. On a regular basis, once or twice a year, you should check the vital signs of your organization. That means doing regular assessments of the internal climate of your business and keeping your finger on the pulse of the paying customer.

Validating the Report Card for Internal Customers

Too many business owners make the mistake of only looking outward, toward the external, paying customer. And, of course, it is important to the success of your business to do that. But keep in mind that validating the report cards of internal customers—your employees and colleagues—is absolutely necessary to deliver extraordinary service to the external customers.

The way to validate the report card of internal customers is by conducting an assessment of the organizational climate of your business. This should be done at least annually. Some businesses check the climate on a quarterly or semiannual basis, using a quick-check method. You could, for example, place an index card with three or four questions on it, in your employee's pay envelopes. Set up collection points for the cards near elevators, restrooms, or the company cafeteria, and ask employees to deposit their cards.

Validating the External Customer Report Card

You should probably plan to conduct focus groups with customers once or twice a year. Depending upon the kind of business you are in and your competitive climate, more frequent focus groups could be in order. A survey of a representative sample of your customers should be done annually, using input from the focus groups to update the questionnaire and to add new factors related to the quality of your service and your product.

Some of the on-the-spot interview techniques we discussed in Chapter 7—opportunistic, telephone, intercept and on-site interviews—can also be used to validate your customer report cards on a regular basis. Eventually, you will want to build a complete *service quality measurement system,* and that is the focus of the next chapter.

CHAPTER 10

BUILDING A SERVICE QUALITY MEASUREMENT SYSTEM

Customers are not constant creatures.

Just when you think you've got them figured out, they change direction. Their motivations, attitudes, beliefs, and values seem predictable and measurable one day and totally incomprehensible the next.

It would be a much easier life for business owners, executives, and managers if customers were unwavering in their loyalty; more appreciative of the efforts exerted by those who serve them; and less demanding in their interactions with service providers.

If only they would let you know in advance when they are beginning to tire of the relationship you've worked so hard to establish with them! If they would just tell you (preferably in a polite and calm manner, when, where, and how you can keep them happy and what you can do to keep service as your driving force.

Some will. But they are, by far, in the minority. You will have to create a means by which you can regularly measure the quality of service you provide to your customers. We call this the Service Quality Measurement System (SQMS).

You need the SQMS not only to stay in touch with the perceptions of your customers, but also as a means of informing employees and managers just how well they are performing in their efforts to deliver quality service. Also, you'll need solid, quantitative data to support performance appraisals of those responsible for the delivery of superior service. Middle managers and supervisors need tangible feedback from customers so they can coach and encourage their employees in areas that need improvement.

MAKING MEASUREMENT A HABIT

It just isn't enough to sample your customers' opinions every few years or so. You need some mechanism in place that will allow you to check their psychological pulse on a consistent and accurate basis. One of the most challenging aspects of managing the quality of service is to create reliable measurements of the customer report card. Marriott keeps close tabs on its customers. Dennis Wagner, vice president of room operations for Marriott, says, "We do several surveys a year to find out what people want. We also ask how they like what we have, and to keep ahead, we ask what they might want in the future."[1] You have to make a habit of measuring your most valuable product: service.

Making measurement a habit is not so difficult as it is demanding. A service-driven organization makes a fetish of knowing its customers and never relinquishes its efforts to find out all it can about all its customers. But that requires a kind of corporate consciousness that keeps everyone's antennae tuned to the signals the customer constantly is broadcasting. Failure to listen when your customer is talking to you can be costly. As one computer manager at a large Southern bank told *Business Week,* "For years we've been telling IBM what we want and they never gave it to us. Now we're listening to what Digital Equipment Corporation (DEC) has to offer."[2]

But listening carefully to the customer and measuring service regularly can pay off handsomely. Disney is a case in point. The corporation received honorable mention in *Business Month* magazine's 1988 selection of the best managed companies in the United States. The theme-park operations, which account for two-thirds of revenues, were up 10 percent over 1987's record of $1.8 billion. Overall, Disney closed the fiscal year ending September 30, 1988 with $3.2 billion in sales and $510 million in profits.[3]

The theme parks make measurement of customer satisfaction a habit. For example, every executive is required to bring his or her family to the park on a day off and spend eight hours as a customer. Then the executive must write a report on what it's like to experience Disneyland from the customer point of view.

Every month, guest reactions are sampled to measure changes in values and demographics. Every executive is expected to spend three hours each week standing in lines, going into shops, and talking to customers. With 12 million paying guests annually passing through its gates, Disney makes a fetish of staying close to its customers.

Along with focusing on the external, paying customer, Disney stays close to its internal customers and makes a habit of measuring service within. A 156 item questionnaire is completed by one half the administrative group and one half the salaried employees every six months.

Another example: Cincinnati Gas and Electric Company (CG&E) has a very short and simple corporate mission: "The Cincinnati Gas and Electric Company will be the best energy *service* company in the United States." Jack Randolph, chief executive officer of CG&E, says, "We must measure whether we are the 'best energy service company in the United States' not by our internal indicators, but from our customer's perspective. Their vote is the one that counts."

To collect and count the votes, Randolph says CG&E surveys its customers twice each year—once in the spring and once in the fall. "We also survey employees and ask them how they think we are doing and what we might be doing differently."

Marriott hotels make it a policy to actively solicit guest feedback in several ways. They're not content to put comment cards in the rooms and hope for the best. If you stay at a Marriott property, you'll probably have the person at the checkout counter ask you whether you've filled one out. If not, he or she will probably ask you to do so. And when the staff asks you "Is everything OK?" chances are they mean it, and will react immediately to any concern you express.

BASIC STRUCTURE FOR A SQMS

It's never too early to begin setting up your SQMS. You'll need several basic components to make it work: data-gathering instruments, a way to interpret your data, and a reporting and analysis mechanism. Also, you'll need to set up means for taking advantage of informal data gathering through the use of point-of-sale feedback, mystery shoppers, and other on-the-spot opportunities to sample customer opinion.

Designing Data-Gathering Instruments

Let's assume you've done the front-end work. Through the focus groups and individual interviews with your various customer constituencies, you've uncovered critical factors of importance to your customers. You've created or commissioned your first surveys—probably one with your internal customers—employees—and another for your external customers.

Most importantly, you've identified those *key service attributes* that make a difference in the mind of the customer, especially when your business is compared one-to-one with your competitors. What remains now is to make the customer report card you've created a regular measurement tool to help managers and employees alike anticipate and adjust to changes in your customers' beliefs, values, attitudes, and behaviors.

The *service attribute matrix* can be used to create a priority of key service attributes. From these attributes you select the *final service criteria*. These criteria will, in all likelihood, become the basis for your SQMS.

John Lauri, chief executive officer of Poudre Valley Hospital (PVH), a large medical center in northern Colorado, says, "Superior service, we believe, is essential to our development as the most respected health care provider in northern Colorado. Providing good customer service takes a lot more than just being courteous, friendly, helpful, and compassionate. It requires that our facilities be designed and maintained with our customers clearly in mind. Maybe we'll discover that a particular document is confusing, or that a hallway sign is difficult to understand. Maybe we'll learn that our computer systems need modification, or that our parking lot should be redesigned. Our intention is to become totally customer-focused, and I believe the management of the hospital must become service management."

To get started, PVH set up a three-tiered service quality measurement system. Here's how it evolved. The first step was an assessment of the physicians who were on staff or who admitted patients to the hospital. A 20 item questionnaire was developed for the physician group. This survey questionnaire was used to identify areas for service improvement among the physician group.

Similarly, a long-needed assessment of the internal climate of the organization was conducted. As part of their new SQMS, all of the employees in the hospital are asked, twice each year, to complete a questionnaire on service matters. As new issues emerge, they are added to the next survey. Items that are no longer relevant are dropped.

Finally, a survey was constructed for patients. The survey is done every six months and assesses the opinions of patients who were admitted to the hospital within the current six month period. A separate survey was constructed for patients who were not admitted, but were treated in the outpatient clinic. The data from these surveys provide the basis for the development of performance appraisals and the development of reward and recognition systems. They help keep the focus on the hospital's commitment to top-quality service.

In addition to this formal data-gathering project, PVH asks each patient to complete a short questionnaire at the conclusion of his or her hospital stay, covering all aspects of the experience. This is an important point. An effective SQMS consists of both formal and informal data-gathering and processing. Surveys and questionnaires are balanced with on-the-spot opportunistic and intercept interviews.

A good blend of statistical and personal data-gathering is done by Club Mediteranee (Club Med). This Paris-based organization invests a tremendous amount of energy in gathering and analyzing customer feedback. Each of the Club's 100 "villages," or resort locations, has a report card compiled from evaluation sheets presented to all guests, or "members," as they are called in Club Med's special language of the escape vacation.

According to chairman Gilbert Trigano, "We have members from all countries of the world visiting our villages. They all have different languages, needs, interests, social values, and personal habits. They all have different preferences for recreation, for service amenities, for personal contact with our staff, and for time structuring. It's important that we understand the diversity of our clientele in order to keep our service products designed for their needs."

His brother, Serge Trigano, goes on to say, "Good customer information is the lifeblood of our business. We are always investigating the differences in how people perceive our type of product."

Club Med uses a sophisticated computer tracking system to measure and feed back customer satisfaction information to each of the villages. Each *chef de village,* or resort manager, receives a regular report of statistical measures of customer evaluation for his or her individual village. Scores cover all aspects of the member's stay. Breakdowns are available by nationality and gender, as well as by department.

In addition to its highly refined tracking system, Club Med relies on its primary member-contact employees, called GO's. A GO is a *gentil organisateur,* or kind of professional socializer whose job is to mingle with members at virtually all hours, and to look after their special needs and interests. These are usually young, energetic, personable people of various nationalities. As part of their jobs, they are expected to keep in touch with member perceptions and needs, and to provide feedback to the *chef de village* about possible improvements in the service.

The Travelers Express Company (TE), located in Minneapolis, provides share draft services to credit unions. TE devised a questionnaire to gather information about three dimensions of customer service: (1) its value to the customer, (2) the quality of service delivered, and (3) the ability of the company to respond to customer needs. The questionnaire was designed to evaluate intangible aspects of service such as promptness, efficiency, and reliability.

Through this service quality measurement system, TE found that their credit union customers valued reliability (completeness and timeliness of reports) and efficiency, but did not give high marks to a systems operations training program which Travelers Express provided. As a result, TE was able to refocus its resources and efforts to more closely match customers' expectations.[4]

Of course, your own version of the SQMS will have to be tailored to the unique characteristics of your business. The goal you're aiming for is the creation of a set of measurement instruments that provide you with a quantitative assessment of your business performance on a regular basis, as well as using the informal contact points with customers to gather important data. When constructing questionnaires, be sure that whatever items you include have been tested with a small pilot group before the questionnaire is used on a large scale.

Getting Customers to Fill Out a Survey

Unless you have a captive group of people, you will have to get your survey into your customers' hands and then hope that they will complete the questionnaire and return it to you. There are some techniques which direct-mail marketers use to get customers to respond to mail offers. Take some time to study the junk mail that you get. Notice the use of color, the size of envelopes, and the message printed on the outside of the envelope. All are designed to get you, the customer, to open the direct-mail piece.

Don Schrello, a direct-marketing expert based in Long Beach, California, says, "You have to use every tool in your kit, every trick of the trade to get a high return rate on surveys or any kind of direct-marketing appeal. A window envelope will net a higher return rate than a regular one. Blue lettering on the envelope increases the return rate, and so does a red mail metering mark instead of a stamp."

You might also consider what the direct-marketing industry calls a *bribe* to get your customer to return the survey. One company encloses a crisp dollar bill with each survey and enjoys an exceptionally high rate of return. You could offer a discount on the next purchase. Domino's, the huge pizza chain, gives customers a 50 percent discount on their next pizza for filling out customer survey slips. The average return rate on Domino's surveys is 80 percent. Phil Bressler, a regional director for Domino's, reads 1,600 customer survey slips every month.[5]

Certainly, you should include a self-addressed, stamped envelope for the respondent to use to return your survey. You can reasonably expect to get back somewhere between 20 and 30 percent of the total number of surveys you send out. Your response may be higher or lower, depending upon the customers you survey and the design of the questionnaire itself.

One rule of thumb is to try to keep things short. Make it easy for the customer to respond. Having a series of letters or numbers to circle is much better than open-end questions for which they have to write out answers.

Guarding Against Response Bias

Response bias means that a certain category of customers is completing your survey questionnaire more frequently than another. For example, if you notice a larger than usual number of responses from customers who are either very happy or very dissatisfied with your service, it might be a good idea to do a "reality check" of the questionnaire.

Select a random sample of customers and have them complete the questionnaire. Check the responses against the pattern of too-high or too-low results you've been getting. There could be something in the way the question is written that is leading respondents to answer negatively or positively more often than they should.

Be careful of demographic bias in the responses. If you notice that a certain age, income, geographic, or political group is consistently returning more or fewer questionnaires than comparable groups, you may want to take a second look at recipients of your questionnaire. You wouldn't, for example, want to mail questionnaires only to non-Hispanic customers if a sizable percentage of the customers you want to survey are Hispanic.

If you're in doubt, try interviewing a group of customers, using the questions as a guide. You'll have the opportunity to listen to the way they interpret the questions. Don't hesitate to edit or change questions if necessary. Just be sure you don't stray away from the *key service attribute* that caused you to ask the question in the first place. You may also need to repeat the focus-group process to be sure you have extracted the correct key service attributes.

In addition to these quantitative studies, it is usually a good idea to look for other ways to get feedback from your customers. Remember, you started with focus groups because you wanted to get inside the customers' heads, and find out what was really important to them. You can begin to gather qualitative, descriptive data that will help support and amplify the responses to your format surveys.

MAKING USE OF INFORMAL FEEDBACK

If you're committed to top quality service, then you need to set up means by which you can get regular, informal feedback from your customers about how you're doing. Bear in mind that what we're going to suggest is not intended as a substitute for the kind of in-depth research we've already described. Focus groups, interviews, and surveys are data collection tools that you use when you plan and execute a formal assessment of your service systems. But during the stretch of time between your formal research projects, you'll need a communication vehicle that will allow you to informally sample customer opinion.

British Airways has taken customer feedback to some surprising levels of sophistication. Travelers passing through London's Heathrow and Gatwick airports are greeted by video feedback stations, which are kiosks equipped with video cameras. The customer can record his or her message about the airline's service directly on video tape, along with facial expressions (and, presumably, gestures as well) in privacy and without having to speak face-to-face with airline employees. British Airway's market researchers then review the tapes and follow up with letters to travelers who include their names and addresses on the video tape.

Don't forget the value of on-the-spot data collection. At the point of sale, during the moment of truth, the customer is usu-

FIGURE 10–1

WE CARE
[C]USTOMERS
[A]RE
[R]EALLY
[E]VERYTHING

PLEASE COMPLETE THIS FORM AND LEAVE IT HERE WITH US WHEN YOU FINISH YOUR SHOPPING TODAY.

THANK YOU FOR GIVING US YOUR COMMENTS AND SUGGESTIONS. WE'RE ALWAYS LOOKING FOR NEW WAYS TO SERVE YOU BETTER.

PALAIS ROYAL

CUSTOMER SERVICE SALESCHECK PALAIS ROYAL

Dear Customer:
  We'd like to hear from you, because how you feel about our performance is very important to us. This is a way that we can learn how to give you the best possible service. After all, satisfying you is our most important function. Thank you for taking the time to help.

PLEASE COMPLETE THIS FORM AND LEAVE IT WITH US WHEN YOU FINISH YOUR SHOPPING.

A. How would you rate the salesperson who sold you this merchandise?
4 ☐ EXCELLENT
3 ☐ GOOD
2 ☐ AVERAGE
1 ☐ POOR

B. How would you rate this salesperson's knowledge of the merchandise?
4 ☐ EXCELLENT
3 ☐ GOOD
2 ☐ AVERAGE
1 ☐ POOR

C. How would you rate this salesperson's promptness in serving you?
4 ☐ EXCELLENT
3 ☐ GOOD
2 ☐ AVERAGE
1 ☐ POOR

D. Did the salesperson thank you by name? ☐ Yes
☐ No

IF YOU USED THE FITTING ROOM PLEASE ANSWER THIS QUESTION:
E. Did the salesperson return to the fitting room while you were still there?
☐ Yes
☐ No

Additional Comments _____
_____
_____

X_____
Customer's Signature

ally more than willing to give an opinion of your service. Look for opportunities to get feedback forms in the hands of your customers.

Palais Royal is a chain of upscale retail clothing stores located in Houston. They attach a short form to each credit card charge slip and ask the customer to complete the card and leave it in the store when they've finished shopping. Collection boxes for the cards are posted in convenient locations throughout their stores. Figure 10–1 shows a copy of the "Customer Service Salescheck" Palais Royal uses.
To gather informal comments, the store also places pads of blank paper and pencils in conspicuous locations, on which customers can write their personal comments about the quality of service.

Figure 10–2 shows a straightforward report card Holiday Inn uses, which is placed in all guest rooms to assess key aspects of its hotel and restaurant operations. Notice the useful demographic data that are gathered.

The W. H. Smith Company operates gift shops in airports. The form shown in Figure 10–3 is placed on the counter near the cash register for customers to pick up. The responses follow an agree-disagree scale and also allow the customers to specify the kind of merchandise they would like to see offered for sale. These forms are typical of survey questionnaires used for informal gathering of customer perception. Such data can add rich qualitative data to your service quality measurement system.

EFFECTIVELY MANAGING CUSTOMER COMPLAINTS

Customer complaints form an important part of your service quality measurement system. It might surprise you to know that most customers who become dissatisfied with your product or service will probably never tell you about it. They'll just go quietly away. You won't have a chance to recover from the incident. However, they will tell numerous people *except* you about the poor treatment they believe they've received at your business.

FIGURE 10–2

BSA
0307 HOLIDAY INN® REPORT CARD

		EXCELLENT			POOR	
		A	B	C	D	F

1. Overall how would you grade *this* Holiday Inn hotel? Please check one. — 1

2. **HOTEL APPEARANCE:** Building Exterior — 2
Lobby/Public Areas/ Recreational Areas — 3

3. **YOUR ROOM:** Price/Value — 4
Appearance — 5
Cleanliness — 6
Bathroom — 7
How well did everything work?* — 8

4. **HOTEL STAFF SERVICE:** Friendliness — 9
Efficiency* — 10
Services (Messages, Wake-up Calls, Bellmen, etc.)* — 11

5. **RESTAURANT:** Price/Value — 12
Food Quality — 13
Service Quality — 14

6. Have you stayed at *this* Holiday Inn hotel before?   ☐ Yes   ☐ No   15

7. (a) If you returned to this vicinity, would you go out of your way to stay at this hotel again?   ☐ Yes   ☐ No   16

   (b) If no, where would you prefer to stay?
   ☐ Another Holiday Inn hotel   ☐ Other Hotel (Please specify) ____   17

8. Reason for trip.   ☐ Business   ☐ Pleasure Personal   18

9. Number of people in room.   ☐ One   ☐ Two or more   19

10. *Comments/suggestions: _____

_____

_____

_____

_____

Date of Stay _____ Room # _____

Your Name / Address _____
(Please)

_____ Zip _____

Phone _____ / _____
(Area Code)

Sacramento-I-80-Northeast, CA 4283

FIGURE 10–3

Customer Service Questionnaire
Your Comments Are Important To Us.

Dear Customer,

Our goal is to provide you the best possible service. Recognizing that sometimes we succeed and other times we fail, we would like to know how well we are doing. Your comments will help us serve you better.

Sincerely,

M. Leon Jensen
President and
Chief Executive Officer

Please Check

	no opinion	strongly agree	agree	disagree*	strongly disagree*
Sales Associates were courteous.	☐	☐	☐	☐	☐
I did not have to wait too long.	☐	☐	☐	☐	☐
Item(s) I wanted to purchase were in stock.	☐	☐	☐	☐	☐
Item(s) I purchased were fairly and reasonably priced.	☐	☐	☐	☐	☐
Store operating hours met my needs.	☐	☐	☐	☐	☐
Sales Associates were quick and efficient at the cash register.	☐	☐	☐	☐	☐

* If you disagree or strongly disagree, please share your viewpoint with us.

_____
_____
_____

Other merchandise I would like to see offered for sale:

_____
_____
_____

Additional remarks and suggestions:

_____
_____

Date of this visit _____

Time of this visit _____ ☐ a.m. ☐ p.m.

Name _____

Address _____

City _____ State _____ Zip _____

Telephone # _____

May we include you on our mailing list? ☐ yes ☐ no

(Please drop in any mailbox. No Postage Necessary.)

Store # 8C9

Technical Assistance Research Programs, Inc. (TARP) is a Washington, D.C.-based research company that specializes in consumer issues. The White House Office of Consumer Affairs commissioned a study of consumer behavior during the Carter administration. TARP discovered some very telling behaviors on the part of customers who complain about products or services:

1. The average business never hears from *96 percent* of its unhappy customers.

2. When a customer has a service problem, he or she will tell at least 9 or 10 other people about it. *Thirteen percent of unhappy customers will tell up to 20 other people about the incident.*

3. For each single complaint it receives, the average company has *26 customers with problems* and at least six of them are "serious."

4. If a customer's complaint is satisfactorily handled, up to 70 percent will do business again with the company that upset them. *If the complaint was also resolved very quickly, 95 percent will return for business.*

5. Customers whose complaints were satisfactorily resolved *will tell up to five people* about the positive treatment they received.[6]

If you are serious about making your business totally customer-focused, you will not just respond to your customers' complaints, you'll actively seek them out. Each complaint represents an opportunity to get better. Our experience has shown there are several types of customers, and each is motivated by different values, attitudes, and beliefs. When they complain, their behaviors reflect these inputs. All of your service delivery people must know how to actively seek complaints and respond to them from various types of customers.

The Meek Customer

This type of person is nonassertive, reticent, and reluctant to complain. Because he or she may be intimidated by the thought of complaining, they usually suffer in silence. They are the ones who comprise that group who won't give you an opportunity to make things right, but just quietly take their business to your competitors.

With the meek customer, it isn't sufficient for the service employee to breeze by with a quick, "Everything OK?" To encourage this customer to tell you if there is a problem with your product or service, you must actively solicit specific information.

It is also essential to note the nonverbal behavior of meek customers, which may reflect their discontent even though they don't mention any problems.

The Aggressive Customer

Just the opposite of the meek customer, this type readily complains—often loudly and at length. Although difficult to deal with, at least you don't have to guess about what went wrong from this customer's point of view.

The danger in dealing with the aggressive customer is that the service employee's own aggression may become "hooked," and the complaint can escalate into outright combat. An incident at the Sir Francis Drake Hotel in San Francisco illustrates how quickly this can happen. A man checking into the hotel was told it was fully booked and that the hotel was putting him up at another very nice hotel across the street. The customer became enraged and began shouting at the desk clerk. The clerk, in turn, threatened to call the police if the man didn't lower his voice. This led to a shouting match between the two of them about the freedom of speech and the legitimacy of one another's ancestry. Well, you get the idea.

Aggressive customers must be allowed to ventilate, that is, to "get it off their chest." They don't respond well to your attempts to provide excuses or reasons the product or service was unsatisfactory. The most productive approach is to let them ventilate, accept what they say without necessarily agreeing that they are right, then tell them what you are going to do in response to the complaint.

The High Roller Customer

High rollers are so named because they expect the best and are willing to pay for it. When they complain, they are likely to do so in a fairly reasonable manner, unless they are a hybrid of both the aggressive and high roller characteristics.

Like the aggressive customer, they aren't particularly interested in excuses. They are interested in results and what you are going to do to recover from the breakdown in product or service quality.

The best approach with the high roller is respectful and active listening, careful questioning to determine the cause of their complaint, and rapid response to fix the situation.

The Rip-Off Customer

In an ideal world all people, both businesspersons and customers, would be completely honest and ethical in their dealings. You know, from experience, that this is not so. There is a small minority of customers whose mission in life is to rip-off your business. They are the ones who will challenge warranties on products and fabricate mistreatment by your employees.

Their goal is not so much to get their complaint satisfied as it is to also "win" by getting something they're not entitled to receive. Something that goes beyond the bounds of adequate and responsive compensation for a failed product or unsatisfactory service.

On the few occasions when your service employees encounter a rip-off customer, they should remain unfailingly polite, use accurate data to back up their response to the customer's complaint, and be certain that the recovery is in keeping with what your company would normally do, given the circumstances. A sure tip-off that you're dealing with the rip-off customer is a constant and repetitive, "Not good enough," response to your efforts to satisfy him or her.

But, in the grand scheme of things, it might be better to accept the fact that when you become a customer-driven organization, you become more vulnerable to this type of customer. What you might lose to these unfair consumers can be regained by the good will and increased business you create with your other customers.

Nordstrom has found this to be true. In their efforts to supply complete customer service, the Nordstrom employee is authorized to accept a return of merchandise without a receipt, even if it cannot be established that the product was actually purchased at Nordstrom. As you might imagine, this opens the door to the occasional rip-off artist.

In California, Nordstrom recently joined in the criminal prosecution of one of these rip-off customers. The man made a living by shoplifting products and then taking them back to various Nordstrom stores for cash refunds. Over a period of two or three years, according to reports, he lived the good life at Nordstrom's expense until he was caught.

But compared to the goodwill and revenue which Nordstrom generates because of its extraordinary customer-centered policies, the loss to the rip-off customers is inconsequential.

The Chronic Complainer

You've met them. They are never satisfied. There is always something wrong with the product or service they have received. Their mission in life is to whine. And yet, they are your customers, too. They can't be dismissed, as frustrating as they are to deal with.

Service employees dislike the chronic complainer more than any other type of customer because all their efforts to redress the service problem seem helpless. Dealing with this type of customer requires extraordinary patience. You have to be willing to listen and to be careful about letting your own anger get aroused as a result of the frustration in dealing with the chronic complainers.

The most productive technique is a sympathetic ear, a sincere apology, and an effort to correct the problem. Most chronic complainers, unlike the rip-off customer, will accept and appreciate your attempts to recover. They want an apology and they appreciate it when they are listened to and given a sense of importance. In spite of their chronic complaining, they tend to be loyal customers and are among those who will tell others of your positive response to their complaints. They're just more frustrating to deal with than anything else.

Failure to manage the complaint process can be costly. The *American Banker* conducts annual surveys of product and service quality as perceived by consumers. In their 1988 report, "How Consumer America Views the Changing Financial Services Industry," they reported that among banking customers who had service problems or complaints, 37 percent said they changed institutions as a result, and 16 percent said they closed an account.[7]

When customers feel their complaints are not taken seriously, they may do more than just take their business elsewhere. Hospitals are paying more attention to risk management these days. For example, Irwin Press, professor of anthropology at the University of Notre Dame, found that hospital patients may become predisposed to sue. According to Press, patients have expectations of how a hospital episode should occur, based on their cultural foundation, such as social class and experiences with illness. These expectations often clash with the hospital's values and organization, resulting in a predisposition to sue.[8]

If complaints go public, irreparable damage may be done to a business's reputation if it doesn't respond to the complaints quickly and effectively. Chrysler Corporation found itself in legal hot water when it was disclosed that the company disconnected odometers of test vehicles that were damaged during testing. These vehicles were then fixed and sold as new. Lee Iacocca, the outspoken president of Chrysler, launched a national campaign in the media. In full-page ads, Iacocca proclaimed, "Testing cars is a good idea. Disconnecting odometers is a lousy idea. That's a mistake we won't make again at Chrysler. Period." A second full-page layout described the problem in detail, and what Chrysler planned to do to redress the mistake.[9] Fast response to consumer complaints and a commitment to make things right helped Chrysler recover its credibility and actually strengthened confidence in its products.

How far should you go in handling your customer's complaints? Of course, that's a judgment call by every business owner. In our opinion, and based on working with quite a number of service companies, we think that service-driven businesses go the extra mile. They do whatever it takes to satisfy their customers and to recover when they fumble the service ball.

Phil Bressler is the manager of 18 Domino's pizza stores in Maryland. Bressler's stores have the lowest customer attrition rate among the Domino chain's 3,800 stores. Bressler will go to extraordinary lengths to satisfy a complaining customer. When a local customer repeatedly complained that his pizza had too little sauce, Bressler dumped more than twice the normal amount on a pizza and delivered it himself to the customer at no charge. The customer still wasn't satisfied, so Bressler said, "Since I can't satisfy you, your pizza is free for the rest of your life." The man still eats about $350 worth of free pizza every year.[10]

USING MYSTERY SHOPPERS

Mystery shoppers can provide a great deal of useful data for your SQMS. A mystery shopper is a person unknown to anyone in your business, who spends a certain amount of time shopping your business and prepares a report on his or her experiences as a customer. But using mystery shoppers has some specific requirements if you hope to generate information that will let you assess customer perception.

A mystery shopper could, theoretically, be anyone you choose. However, most businesses use mystery shoppers who are trained in customer perception research. While you could certainly get useful information by having a friend or acquaintance do the mystery shopping, a trained observer can zero in on the specific service attributes you want to find out about.

A trained mystery shopper will begin to assess your business from the very first impression he or she receives until the last contact before leaving your business. Peebles is a chain of department stores spread along the Eastern seaboard of the United States. The company recently acquired the Harvey's chain of department stores in Tennessee and Kentucky. Using mystery shoppers as part of their service quality measurement system has helped the chain make significant service improvements in recent years. W. S. Peebles, III, the company's chairman, says, "All things being equal, our success depends very largely on how we treat our customers. We spend millions of dollars on merchandise, advertising it, and presenting it in our stores, yet we really don't have anything that a customer could not find somewhere else. The only way we've lasted over 90 years in this very competitive business is by providing a sincere, genuine service and appreciation to our shoppers."

Remember, a mystery shopper's experiences, even if reported by one trained in customer perception research, is only one person's perspective. Like the focus group research we discussed earlier, mystery shopper data is qualitative and must be validated by a carefully designed and tested measurement process.

PRODUCING USABLE REPORTS

Having an effective service quality measurement system in place is one thing. Making use of what you find out is another. That's why you need to put all the data you collect from your SQMS into some kind of usable form.

When you become a customer-focused organization you need to get into the report card generation business in a big way. Every month, at least, there should be some kind of message going throughout the organization that says, "Well folks, here's what our customers thought of us this month." Everyone in a service business needs to have access to this customer report card on a regular basis. As we've noted, the factors on the report card change over time, and it's important for your people to stay up to speed on what's happening in the customers' minds.

One of the biggest mistakes we see committed, when a business wants to make service its driving force, is the lack of attention on the part of key management people. You will want to keep the customer information on the front burner at all times. Every management meeting should include, as part of a standing agenda, the discussion of the quality of service data that your SQMS develops for you.

Customer information must be seen as a valuable asset to the organization. Employees need to be rewarded when the data show significant improvement on service issues. And when the report card is not so good, they must be encouraged to do better through positive reinforcement from the frontline managers.

Some businesses like to create a special report that contains only the service related information. A special newsletter could be created that both presents current customer information and also recognizes those departments and individuals who are working to make a difference with their customers, both internal and external.

And don't overlook the power of visual communication. Many businesses have video capabilities now. They can be an effective and efficient means of relaying customer data to the employees, especially those who may be in satellite or field offices.

Videotaping a few interviews with customers and showing segments to your employees is an effective way to bring customer perceptions to life. If there is a special meeting where customers are present, use the opportunity to interview some of them. Plum Creek Timber Co., with headquarters in Seattle, is the country's 15th largest timber management business, with annual sales in excess of $300 million. The company invites three of its major retail customers to an annual meeting of the firm's top management group. Key managers from all aspects of the firm's operations have an opportunity to ask questions in an open forum with some of their most important clients. Occasions like this are naturals for videotaping and for distribution throughout the company.

The Public Service Company of Colorado, an investor-owned gas and electric utility in Denver, routinely produces videotapes on key issues facing customers and plays them in continuous play sequences in kiosks placed near the company cafeteria, where employees can stop and view them.

Look for unique and creative ways to create reports of customer perception research. You don't have to rely only on written documents. To the extent you can make the information come alive and have relevance to your employees, you increase the usefulness and applicability of the data your service quality measurement system generates.

NOTES

1. *OAG Frequent Flyer,* May 1987, p. 43.
2. *Business Week,* March 30, 1987, p. 86.
3. *Business Month,* December 1988, p. 51.
4. *Marketing News,* April 24, 1987, pp. 13–18.
5. John Hillkirk, "Domino's Service No Game," *USA Today,* July 1987, p. 7.
6. Karl Albrecht and Ron Zemke, *Service America: Doing Business In the New Economy* (Homewood, Ill.: Dow Jones-Irwin, 1985), p. 6.
7. *The Denver Post,* May 1988, p. 4.
8. *Hospitals,* Nov. 1986, p. 52.
9. *U.S. News and World Report,* July 13, 1987, pp. 48–49.
10. Hillkirk, *USA Today.*

CHAPTER 11

CLOSING THE LOOP

We've covered a lot of ground. If you've stayed with us this far, you're probably pretty serious about getting close to your customers and finding out what makes them tick. What remains is to make use of what you know.

One of the lessons we've learned about service management is that it takes a special effort for companies to "walk the talk." Putting what you know to use requires that you make the management of customer perception research as vital to the organization as the profiles you generate to track the financial health of the organization.

If you spend the time and money it takes to do really top-notch customer research, it just doesn't make sense to allow this valuable tool for your business to go unused. We'd like to close the loop of this book by suggesting there are five major ways to put to use what you find out about your customers:

1. Selling better.
2. Delivering better.
3. Recovering better from mistakes.
4. Building better systems.
5. Attracting and keeping better employees.

SELLING BETTER

When you know what's on your customers' report cards, you have the most valuable information in the world. You have the inside track on what motivates your buyer, what his or her attitudes, beliefs, and values are, and how they drive buying behavior. This is the information you need to differentiate your business from that of your competitors.

The data you obtain from your research will allow you to create a service strategy that makes sense for your business and for your customers. By incorporating your customer report card information into your strategy for delivering service, you create one or more unique features that have market value.

A service strategy built upon solid customer information has two useful aspects that will allow you to sell better. First, you can use the data from your customers to chart the course of your business. Decisions you make about product line and what you are going to sell and to whom will be based upon what you know is vital to the customers in your market. Second, the strategy will allow you to create and make public a *service promise* that can create a noticeable difference between your business and that of your competitors.

What is the Service Promise?

A service promise is a guarantee to your customers. A product guarantee, of course, promises that a piece of equipment or an appliance will perform as it should. Well, a service guarantee promises your customers that they are going to be *treated in a special way* when they do business with you. A service promise ensures the customer that the interaction he or she experiences in your place of business will be better than the treatment they can receive anywhere else. Service promises are either *implicit* or *explicit.*

An *implicit service promise* is one that is not published openly where customers can see it, but is demonstrated by the actions of service employees whenever a moment of truth takes place. When a service employee tells a customer, "Now if that doesn't fit or if you change your mind, don't hesitate to bring it back to me," an implicit service promise has been made. If you can imagine a cartoon balloon over the employee's head which represents his or her thoughts, it might say, "It'll be OK if you bring that merchandise back—I'll be glad to help you." The employee's nonverbal communication and actions all add evidence to the implicit service promise.

While Nordstrom does not necessarily post a service promise, its reputation for delivering extraordinary service is well
known. It is implicit in the experience of shopping at
Nordstrom.

An *explicit service promise* is stated overtly. It is published
in some public forum, such as, posters on the wall of your business or in your advertising material. It spells out, in detail,
what the customer can expect when he or she does business
with you. Here is an example of an explicit service promise by
the AMC movie theater chain. In every AMC theater, in a
prominent place in the lobby, is a sign with the service promise
shown in Figure 11–1.

Using what you know to sell better requires you to manage
the service promise to your customers, whether it is implicit or
explicit. It does no good to make a service promise you can't
keep.

One of the ways that the Domino's pizza chain has differentiated itself from its competition is by its 30 minute guaranteed delivery time. If the pizza arrives after 30 minutes the
price is discounted. Along with the time guarantee, Domino's
also guarantees the product quality.

The Santa Clara Medical Center, a Kaiser Permanente fa-
cility, is, to our knowledge, one of the few medical centers in

FIGURE 11–1

> ### Customer Service Guarantee
> - Your viewing environment will be comfortable, the picture will
> be clear, and the sound will be of excellent quality.
> - The theatre complex, particularly the auditoriums and rest-
> rooms, will be clean and attractive.
> - Our employees will be courteous, friendly, and available to
> assist you during your visit.
> - If your AMC movie experience falls short of these guarantees,
> please ask for the Manager of this complex.

Reprinted by permission.

the country that has posted an explicit service guarantee to its patients. The service promise in Figure 11–2 is displayed throughout the medical center's hospital and clinics where it can be easily seen by all customers.

The telephone numbers and names of the medical center administrator, Thomas Seifert, and the physician-in-chief, Christopher Chow, M.D., are listed at the bottom of the Santa Clara service promise. Numerous customers have contacted the medical center and to date, over 300 service improvements have been made from both employee and patient suggestions.

Because service promises are based upon what customers say is important to them, the organization that stays close to its customers and keeps up to date on the report card is the one that is going to be in an advantaged position. But you wouldn't want to make a service promise if you were not prepared to deliver on that promise. On a national scale, Kaiser Permanente began running commercials on national network television, promising a "personal physician."

Hoping to gain a competitive edge over other HMO's, the company created a series of elegant commercials featuring ac-

FIGURE 11–2

Our Promise to you, our Health Plan Members

In every encounter, with every person, in every part of our organization you will experience:

- *Confidence* in the quality of care you receive.
- *Caring,* courteous and prompt service in your interactions with physicians and staff members.
- *Convenience* as you use our system.
- *Confidentiality* and respect for your medical information and condition.

If at any time you believe we are not living up to this Service Promise, please contact us at (phone number).

Reprinted by permission.

tual Kaiser physicians. The commercials were well done and technically superior. The closing line for each spot was, "At Kaiser Permanente, you can have a physician like Dr. Mary Jones." However, the performance of the organization in delivering this implied promise was erratic throughout the corporation's 12 national regions.

Market Value of the Service Promise

You can sell better when you can publicly promise your customers a level of treatment that your competitors are unwilling or unable to match. And, even more importantly, a strong service promise may allow you to capture a larger share of your market or charge a higher price for your product.

Some companies have created customer "Bill of Rights" proclamations that include explicit service promises. The Latrobe Area Hospital, a nonprofit hospital located in Latrobe, Pennsylvania, publishes a 22-statement Patients' Bill of Rights. The document specifies, explicitly, what the patient can expect as a customer of the hospital from the doctors, nurses, and support staff.

Quentin McKenna, president of Kennametal Corporation, prides himself on Kennametal's Customer Bill of Rights:

1. The customer has a right to get exactly what he ordered.
2. The right to receive the product when it was promised.
3. The right to receive value for his money.
4. The right to be told the truth.
5. The right to buy from whomever he chooses.

Chrysler Corporation's chairman, Lee Iacocca, has recently made a number of television appearances announcing his Customer Bill of Rights, which specifies the expectations a customer is entitled to in purchasing a Chrysler product.

The Quill Corporation, a national supplier of office products and supplies, includes a Bill of Rights in all its catalogs. Notice that the statements shown in Figure 11–3 include explicit promises as to how the Quill Customer will be treated.

FIGURE 11–3

As a Quill Customer, you can hold these truths to be self-evident...

Our Quill Customers' Bill of Rights states our basic beliefs on how we should run our company. We have followed them from the first day we began doing business 32 years ago.

THE QUILL CUSTOMERS'

BILL of RIGHTS

Restated and approved at Lincolnshire, Illinois on Friday, the First of January, One Thousand Nine Hundred and Eighty-eight.

The undersigned officers and the more than 950 employees of Quill Corporation express a desire to clearly state the principles and ideals which guide all of us at Quill in our relationship with our customers.

We feel this unusual step is necessary at this time because we find ourselves when we are customers... both as individuals and as a company... frequently dissatisfied with the way we are treated. Disinterest, discourteousness, bad service, late deliveries and just plain bad manners are too common.

We can't tell others how to run their businesses (except by not buying from them). But we can and will run Quill as we feel a business should be run. Therefore, the following is a list of what we consider are the inalienable rights of our customers. *We expect to be held to account whenever we deny any of these rights to any customer.*

1. As a customer, you are entitled to be treated like a real, individual, feeling Human Being... with friendliness, honesty and respect.

2. As a customer, you are entitled to full value for your money. When you buy a product you should feel assured that it was a good buy and that the product is exactly as it was represented to be.

3. As a customer, you are entitled to a *complete* guarantee of satisfaction. This is especially true when you buy the product sight unseen through the mail or over the phone.

4. As a customer, you are entitled to fast delivery. Unless otherwise indicated, the product should be shipped within 8-32 hours. In the event of a delay, you are entitled to immediate notification, along with an honest estimate of expected shipping date.

5. As a customer, you are entitled to speedy, courteous, knowledgeable answers on inquiries. You are entitled to all the help we can give in finding exactly the product or information needed.

6. As a customer, you are entitled to the privilege of being an individual and of dealing with individuals. If there is a question on your account, you are entitled to talk with or correspond with another *individual* so the question can be resolved immediately on the most mutually satisfactory basis possible.

7. AS A CUSTOMER, YOU ARE ENTITLED TO BE TREATED EXACTLY AS WE WANT TO BE TREATED WHEN WE ARE SOMEONE ELSE'S CUSTOMER.

Jack Miller
President

Harvey L. Miller
Secretary

Arnold Miller
Treasurer

We first published this Bill of Rights in 1970 when we had 32 officers and employees. As we reprint it here today, we've grown to more than 950 employees. We believe that respecting your rights as a customer has helped us grow to this size.

Note also that the graphic treatment is congruent with the notion of a quill; this is good use of a visual metaphor with a historical connection.

Money Back Guarantees

Explicit service promises also include those that guarantee satisfaction with the product. Using their easy-to-return policies and hassle-free methods for returning the customer's money, these companies sell better. They've used what they know about their customers to create product and service promises that make a difference in the market place.

Lands' End is a mail-order catalogue company located in Dodgeville, Wisconsin (population 3,458). The company does about $30 million per year in sales with customers it rarely sees. Nine million people receive the Lands' End catalogue every month, and 45 per cent of them make purchases in a six month period. In Figure 11–4 we've reprinted a copy of the Lands' End unconditional guarantee. The implicit promise in this guarantee is that you will receive superior service treatment because you are a Land's End customer. The explicit promise is that merchandise can be returned at any time for any reason for a full refund.

Direct mail experts say the guarantee is one of the most critical elements of the selling message, because the customer can't see the actual product in advance. Prominent, confidence inspiring guarantees, displayed well and repeated, make a big difference in mail order response. And, if your product line is good, your return rate should be very small; so the guarantee really costs very little.

L.L. Bean, Inc., in Freeport, Maine, has a long history of no-strings-attached service and product guarantees. A good example of a service strategy and promise is the one found on an L.L. Bean circular from 1912, shown on the top of page 216.

L.L. Bean's "Golden Rule" was, "Sell good merchandise at a reasonable profit, treat your customers like human beings, and they'll always come back for more." The L.L. Bean company often cites that statement in its advertising and catalog

FIGURE 11–4

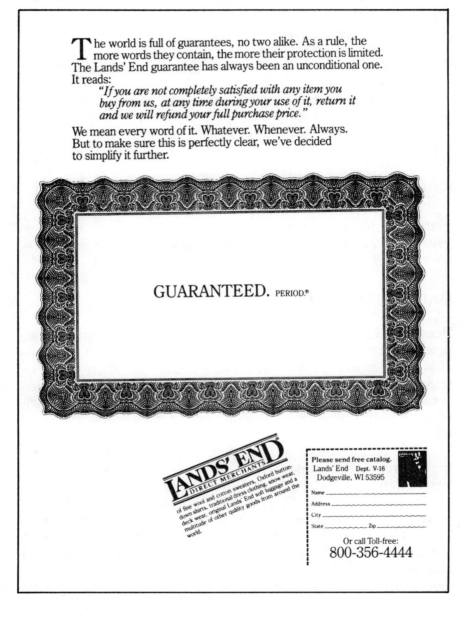

The world is full of guarantees, no two alike. As a rule, the more words they contain, the more their protection is limited. The Lands' End guarantee has always been an unconditional one. It reads:

"If you are not completely satisfied with any item you buy from us, at any time during your use of it, return it and we will refund your full purchase price."

We mean every word of it. Whatever. Whenever. Always. But to make sure this is perfectly clear, we've decided to simplify it further.

GUARANTEED. PERIOD.®

Please send free catalog.
Lands' End   Dept. V-16
Dodgeville, WI 53595

Name
Address
City
State _____ Zip _____

Or call Toll-free:
800-356-4444

NOTICE

I do not consider a sale complete until goods are worn out and customer still satisfied.

We will thank anyone to return goods that are not perfectly satisfactory.

Should the person reading this notice know of anyone who is not satisfied with our goods, I will consider it a favor to be notified.

Above all things we wish to avoid having a dissatisfied customer.

L. L. Bean

---

materials. In addition, the company has a 24-hour, 365-day-a-year toll free number so customers can reach a customer service representative or sales associate at any time.

DELIVERING BETTER

Becoming customer-focused means you can deliver your service product better. What do we mean by that? We mean you'll be able to place your product or service where and when your customers want them. You'll be able to deliver what you do in such a way that it meets your customers' expectations. Your knowledge of your customers will help you create systems that will truly put them first.

One public sector organization that has made a surprisingly strong commitment to a customer-first service orientation is London's Metropolitan Police Department, better known as Scotland Yard. Sir Peter Imbert, commissioner of "London Metro" as it's more commonly known outside of Hollywood, says, "I believe all public sector organizations must focus on service. That's what we're all about. Certainly we have to deal aggressively and uncompromisingly with lawbreakers, but most of the citizens of London are not lawbreakers. They're the general public, and they deserve the best peacekeeping services we have to give."

Imbert's mission is to manage the contributions of some 40,000 people—28,000 of whom are uniformed police officers—to meet established social objectives. His predecessor, Sir Kenneth Newman, instituted a "policing by objectives" theme of governance in the department, based on a careful analysis of the changing nature of the metropolitan London community, and his organization's role in it. After extensive surveys and investigation of public opinion about the image of the department, Scotland Yard instituted an extensive process of strategy formulation and management planning keyed to the desired role for the organization.

Scotland Yard conducts an annual public opinion survey and a careful investigation of new service issues. According to Imbert, "This kind of information points up some obvious trends and service issues we need to get ready for. The increasing number of senior citizens, for example, means we will be called upon to provide more of certain kinds of services and some new ones not considered before. These and many other findings about our 'customers' have led us to reorganize the department toward fewer layers of management and more of a 'concentric' structure for greater flexibility."

Again, this is a good example of actually *doing something* with customer research information.

Richard Thalheimer founded The Sharper Image, with virtually no capital. Sometimes referred to as "the Gadget King," Thalheimer started the company in 1976 with a $200 investment. Today, he mails 30 million catalogs each year, in which he promotes an average of 150 products. The company's main vehicle of delivery is their catalog, which sells for a dollar at newsstands. It looks like a high-gloss magazine and nets 1.5 orders for each 100 catalogs mailed, each order averaging $130.

A lesson Thalheimer has learned is that you must know your customer and put what you know to work. In an interview with Carol Isaac Barden of *Profiles, Inc.,* he told of the time he ordered 10,000 home gymnasium units, only to find that customers hated them. He also failed in his attempts to publish a women's catalog. Thalheimer says, "It told me I don't know anything about what women like." He also lost money on another lemon, a theft-proof briefcase. "People were afraid the alarm would go off in an important meeting," he says.

Now Thalheimer delivers better because he puts what he's learned to work. The policy at The Sharper Image is that *anything* can be returned, no questions asked, for a full refund and The Sharper Image pays return postage.[1]

Federal Express is another good example of delivering better. Legendary for its couriers' efforts to deliver packages to remote and difficult locations, Federal Express has put its knowledge of its customers to work in order to deliver its service product better. The proliferation of competing companies is testimony to Federal Express' success.

And the effect was not lost on the U.S. Postal Service, which instituted its overnight delivery only after the commercial ventures like Federal Express and United Parcel Service were up and running. In a continuing effort to catch up, the Postal Service now offers to pick up express mail from customers' business locations within two hours.

Delivering better means you have to know what your customers want. That's been our message throughout this book. *The Denver Post* and the *Rocky Mountain News* are the two major competing newspapers in Colorado. In response to customer complaints about spotty delivery and to competition from the *Rocky Mountain News,* the *Post* recently began publishing a service promise in the form of a new delivery guarantee, shown in Figure 11–5.

Delivering better isn't limited to those companies who have a physical product to send out like The Sharper Image, Lands' End, or L.L. Bean. Even if you are a small business owner whose customers purchase on-site in your store, you can still use what you know about them to deliver your product or service better than your competition.

Take a look at your customer data. Are your customers telling you they want merchandise displayed in a certain way? Is there something you could do to make it easier for customers to get into and out of your place of business? How can you make the customer's experience of moving through your business operation as pleasant and easy as possible? All of

FIGURE 11–5

OUR GUARANTEE TO YOU
HOME DELIVERY
BY 6 A.M. WEEKDAYS · BY 7 A.M. WEEKENDS

Dear Reader,

Good Service. A lot of companies pay lip service to the notion. Here at The Post, we're giving it a little more attention than that.

Maybe you're one of our customers who likes to read The Post before heading off to work every morning. You expect us to be there. So, here's a promise:

We commit to you that if you get up early, we'll be there early, too, with a nice, dry, readable newspaper about Denver, the suburbs, the Front Range, Colorado, the Rocky Mountain Empire — and all the news of our nation and our world.

Oh, by the way, we bill by mail now, but we're new at this and need to work harder to provide you with trouble-free billing. So, we'd like to hear from you on this matter, too. For example, if your name is misspelled or the total is wrong, let us know and we'll send you a little gift - and we'll do whatever it takes to correct the mistake on your next bill.

We understand, really understand, how important it is to give our readers good service. After all, if it weren't for you, we wouldn't have much to write about, would we?

Please call 825-7678 any day of the week from 6 a.m. to 7 p.m., weekends from 7 a.m. to 3 p.m., and tell us your concerns. We're here to serve you — 365 days a year!

Thank you,

Moe Hickey

Maurice "Moe" Hickey
Publisher

THE DENVER POST
Voice of the Rocky Mountain Empire

---

these are important ways to improve service by delivering better.

Consider the face-to-face aspect of delivery. Your customer information may tell you that your service-delivery employees need work on their interpersonal skills or on the way they manage their personal grooming. Are they conscious of customers' needs? Do they know how to "read" your customers so that service problems can be headed off in advance? These are concerns of delivery as much as the physical moving of your product from point A to point B.

RECOVERING BETTER FROM MISTAKES

When you put to use what you know about your customers, you'll be in a much better position to recover from mistakes. And they're going to happen. What customers in general want, when a mechanical system of some kind breaks down, is a warm, live human being to make things right. How do you recover when your systems fail? What plan of action do you have as a back-up in case things don't go as they're supposed to? If you're smart, you back up all your computer data in the event the system crashes. No less should be done in terms of the systems serving your customers.

Remember, when customers complain about something, they are giving you a chance to recover better from mistakes. And knowing your customers in the depth and context in which we've been discussing them throughout this book will allow you to recover from your service errors quicker and more effectively.

Take another look at the notice L.L. Bean posted in his store in 1912. He actively solicited complaints and stated in advance his wish to recover from mistakes as quickly as possible in order to avoid having a dissatisfied customer. That's putting to use what you know about your customers, and it's as true today as it was in 1912.

The Commerce Bank in Aurora, Colorado, near Denver, is a small, independent bank with assets of $42 million and an interesting approach to catching mistakes. They pay their customers $5 for each mistake they spot. In the first four months of the program, the bank only had to pay out $80. Other banks have set up rewards for customers who find mistakes, including the National Bank of Detroit, First Wyoming Bank in Cheyenne, Maryland National Bank in Baltimore, and Bank of America in San Francisco. Knowing that their customers' trust and confidence are at stake and that accuracy is a prime factor on the bank customers' report cards, these financial institutions are putting what they know about their customers to work.

BUILDING BETTER SYSTEMS

A key lesson we've learned in our work in service management is that systems are often the enemy of service. Every business, whether large or small, must have systems in order to operate. Some systems are imposed by regulatory bodies and there's not much you can do about them. But it is possible that some of your organization's systems serve the company more than they serve the customer.

When you get to know your customer intimately, you can target systems for change. We mentioned in Chapter 2 the four key systems that will need attention: management, rules and regulations, technical, and social. Using what you find out about your customers will allow you to target these systems for service improvements.

Figure 11-6 shows the System Assessment Model for assessing organizational systems. You might want to use it to identify the relative levels of customer and employee "friendliness" or "unfriendliness" in your systems.

A system is considered customer-friendly if it makes it easy for the customer to get his or her needs met. The same is true for an employee-friendly system. It is one that allows the employee to deliver extraordinary service. It's important to note the strong points in your systems because you might be able to apply their features to other systems that need to be made friendlier to customers. Your systems are unfriendly if they impede the employee or the customer during the moment of truth.

To use this model, just rate each of your customer-impact systems one at a time. Put an X in the proper box in Figure 11–6 for the customer and for the employees. Check with your customers and employees to find out whether your evaluations are correct.

You might want to have your employees use a version of this assessment model to make note of any system problems they encounter when working with customers. Also, use the data you obtain from your customer report card to check which systems may need repair. Make a brief note in the appropriate

FIGURE 11–6 System Assessment Model

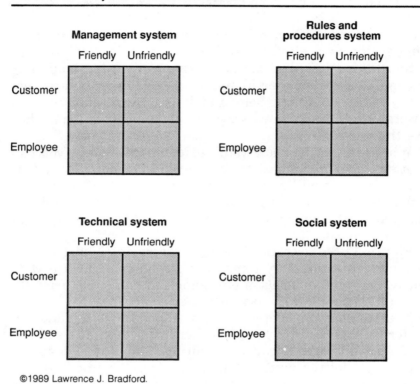

©1989 Lawrence J. Bradford.

quadrant for each system, and you'll create a series of targets to aim at for systems improvement.

The Society of Teachers of Family Medicine (STFM) met recently in Tucson. The members of the STFM are physicians who teach the specialty of family practice to medical students and residents. One of the physicians reported how his university medical center created a better system to solve a serious parking problem. Because the patient care center was located in a large university, there were very few parking places near the center that were not reserved for university officials and faculty members. As a result, patients had to either park several blocks away from the medical center and walk, or have a friend or relative drop them off at the center's entrance.

The chairman of the medical school decided the parking system was not customer-friendly. He knew that an attempt to rearrange parking spaces would not sit well with the university. So he created *valet parking* for the medical center's patients. He hired undergraduate students to drive patients' cars to the remote parking lot and to pick them up when the patient or family member was ready to leave. The students made extra money, and the patients no longer had to park in inconvenient locations. The chairman estimated the valet parking cost the medical school $500 per month, which was more than recaptured by the increase in patient load, as word spread that the parking problem had been solved.

Not all system problems are so easily fixed. Some require substantial outlays of time and capital. But you can be sure that if you base your systems improvements upon what you know about your customers, you'll be targeting those systems that really matter in the customers' perceptions.

ATTRACTING AND KEEPING BETTER EMPLOYEES

We've been impressed by the overall willingness of most service employees to put their customers first. But at times they can be like the little girl in the nursery rhyme: When they are good, they are very, very good, but when they are bad, they are horrid. Knowing your customers increases the chances that your service employees can be very, very good most of the time.

There are five major areas involving employees where you can put to use what you know about your customers: selection, orientation, training, evaluation, and recognition. Knowing what's important to customers will guide you in each of these major areas, as it did for National Westminster Bank of London.

National Westminster Bank of London (NatWest) discovered the importance of selling employees on the concept of putting customers first. "We originally began with a standards approach," says Paul Goodstadt, director of service quality. "We keyed in on employee job standards which we felt were important to good service. But it really wasn't getting us anywhere. We weren't seeing the energy and enthusiasm we'd hoped for. Then we discovered Karl Albrecht's book, *Service America!* and it started us thinking in terms of the customer interface and in terms of the service culture we would need to foster in order to make service quality our competitive weapon."

NatWest built a remarkable service quality program on good customer knowledge and an appeal to employees to do their best for their customers. Says Goodstadt, "Once we had the basic customer information and the quality framework in place, we took the customer-first message to all the people in the organization." NatWest provided a one-day training and communication experience for every single employee—58,000 of them. The company built four special training centers in different parts of the United Kingdom to carry out the massive training program in a record five months. According to Goodstadt, "Once our people saw how big this thing was, and the word got out that the managing director and his senior staff were sitting right next to counter clerks at the very first training session, things really started to pop. People got switched on like never before."

Let's take a closer look at the process of attracting and keeping better employees.

Selection

Careful selection is the first step. Use your customer data to help you pick the right people in the first place, and you won't have service problems later on. If you use your customer report card as a guide, you can begin to select employees who will make a difference in the eyes of your customers.

If your customer perception data tell you that your customers value a lot of personal contact with service representatives, then it doesn't make sense to hire people who are unwilling or unable to work well with others, regardless of their technical skills. Knowing what is important to your customers is critical in selecting the right person for the right job in service industries. Whether you are a small business owner or you work in a huge corporation, the principle is still true.

Selecting the kind of person that will meet your customers' needs in an extraordinary way requires extraordinary knowledge of your customers' expectations. Will this person manage the hundreds of moments of truth in a way that will set your business apart from others like it?

Most employee selection is done from the perspective of the organization, not from the point of view of what customers want when they encounter employees face-to-face. Disneyland hires young people by interviewing them in groups of three. The interviewer notes which candidates smile spontaneously and genuinely react positively to the other two candidates. Because Disneyland's product is "happiness," they hire only those people they feel confident will help them live up to that customer perception. And each person selected for employment is put through an intensive orientation and training program to prepare them to become a cast member in the Disneyland show.

Orientation

Once you've chosen the right people for the right jobs, it's important to give them an in-depth orientation to your service strategy. New employees need to become immersed in the culture of your organization as soon as possible.

Most businesses do a mediocre to poor job of employee orientation, if they do it at all. Rarely do they include information from the customer report card as a basis for creating effective orientation classes for new employees. Seldom are employees exposed to the stories and heroes of the company—those who founded it and who were the original employees—so that they begin to feel a part of the culture themselves.

Again, Disneyland is an interesting example. One of the first experiences an employee has is the presentation of his or her name badge. It doesn't say "Trainee" on it, and it's not some left over badge with the new employee's name written on a piece of tape. It's just like everyone else's—first name only—and it's the same size and shape as the managers' or executives' name badges.

Secondly, the new Disneyland employee is shown a scratchy, black and white kinescope from the original live telecast of opening day of Disneyland, complete with all the foulups, outtakes, and mistakes that were made when the park opened for business on that first day in 1955. Of course, Walt Disney is in the center of things, talking about the park and his dream of creating a place where adults can become children again and where children can enter a magical kingdom. By the time the new cast member at Disneyland is finished with orientation, he or she is already well on the way to becoming the kind of employee who takes a personal interest in seeing that customers' expectations about "The Happiest Place On Earth" are met.

Even if you own a small business, you have a history and culture. Your new employees need to become immersed in your culture. They also need to know what is on your customers' report cards—the things that matter—and the moments of truth they are going to have to manage. They need to know your service strategy—inside and out—and what their role is in delivering on that strategy to their customers.

Training

Using what you know about your customers may be most critical when it comes to training your employees and managers. When you think of all the many kinds of training your employees could receive, it makes sense, in a customer-focused business, to be sure that a healthy portion of that training is based upon what you've come to learn about your customers, and that the skills taught in training programs can actually be applied to create improved grades on your customers' report cards.

It's important to understand the difference among *training, education,* and *development* activities. The last thing you want to do is to invest a lot of time and money in activities that might not produce any lasting results.

Here's the distinction: training helps people learn skills they can apply immediately on the job. Training can be measured and it can be evaluated. Education helps people learn skills they can apply in some *future* application. They probably can't apply the skills immediately, but they most certainly will at some future, designated point. For instance, you show people how to use a new computer software program, but if the new software won't be available for six months, then you've provided an educational, not a training, experience. They can't actually apply the newly learned skills until they can get their hands on the software. You can measure educational events and evaluate them, but *only after the learned skills are applied in the future.* The final point, development, is also a learning experience. It is different from training and education because it may or may not ever be applied on the job, and it is often difficult to measure the skills learned and to evaluate the worth of the program. Development learning experiences are almost always good for people. They are enriching and help people live better lives. Many motivational programs fall into this category. Whether what people learn will be applied on the job or not is left pretty much up to them.

In service management, be sure that the training you provide your people is really training and can be put to work immediately to improve your service product.

The best starting point in training employees to put customers first is to share the information you've gathered through your service quality measurement system about customer perceptions. It is essential that every person in the organization, experienced and newcomer alike, learn what is on your customers' report cards.

Evaluation

It's not enough to just equip people with the skills they need to deliver the kind of service that will create market differentiation for your business. You have to evaluate their efforts, and give them feedback on how they're doing. That's where using what you know about customers really comes into play.

Eventually, service management must become part of employee and manager performance appraisals. This will require the establishment of standards which specify the level of quality you expect from your workforce. And the standards themselves are not enough. You will have to put into place some measurable behaviors that will be evidence that your people are living up to the standards of service which your customers expect.

Setting up service standards and measurable behaviors can be an excellent way to develop teamwork in your organization. Managers, supervisors, and employees can sit down together, use the customer feedback information you've developed, and create service-based performance appraisal systems. Encouraging employees to take part in setting the standards and behaviors is crucial. If you only have management design them and impose them on the workforce, you won't get the results you need. You'll get "rehearsed allegiance," that is, the people will cooperate, but they won't necessarily make a commitment to providing superior service.

Think about the difference between cooperation and commitment the next time you sit down to a breakfast of ham and eggs. The chicken cooperated in the venture, but the pig made a commitment.

Recognition

Even the most dedicated, loyal, and high-performing employee or manager needs to be recognized when he or she goes to extra lengths to put customers first. And we're not only talking about a paycheck. Everyone wants recognition in one form or other. Money can be a great temporary motivator, but it won't have a lasting effect. You need to come up with a set of methods to reward and recognize those individuals who meet the service management challenge in extraordinary ways.

You've probably heard enough about the importance of personal praise and thanking employees for doing a good job. That's a given. Start looking for additional ways to recognize your people that cost little or no money: leaving a personal note on their desk, taking them for a cup of coffee, bringing in refreshments for the group, or ordering a pizza at an odd time of the day are all small ways to let employees and managers know that *you* know they are doing superior work.

And, occasionally, there needs to be a big reward. Maybe you select the outstanding employees who have excelled in their service efforts in a given quarter, and host a nice dinner in a fine restaurant for them and their spouses or guests. Or perhaps you have a drawing once a year or so to select the "employee of the year" for outstanding service. The prize could be something special like a leather briefcase, a weekend at a nice resort, or a trip, depending upon your budget. Santa Clara Medical Center in California awards employees with a coupon that can be redeemed in the hospital cafeteria for a free soft drink. A small thing, surely, but one that gives the employee tangible recognition on the spot for providing extraordinary service. And, the coupons are then put into a drawing with the winner and his or her significant other receiving a nice trip.

Steamboat Ski Corporation, located in Steamboat, Colorado, attracts skiers from throughout the United States and is well known for its friendly, family-centered environment. The resort has a very successful program called "Mountain Magic" that provides instant recognition of employees who go out of their way to provide extraordinary service to the ski resort's customers. Customers are selected at random when they purchase their lift tickets and are given an envelope. Inside the envelope is a certificate that can be redeemed for $10. The customer is invited to give the certificate to any employee in the resort who provides superior service. Hans Geier, president of the resort, says, "The Mountain Magic program has been the best way we've discovered to reward and recognize our employees. The majority of them are seasonal workers, here only for the winter ski season, so we had to come up with a program that would provide an instant and tangible reward for employees who go out of their way for our customers. We're known as the friendliest ski resort in the country, and we intend to hold on to that honor." In a recent survey, the Mountain Magic program was listed as one of the top benefits employees receive.

Don't overlook the value of peer recognition. Being selected by your peers for your extra efforts to put customers first has a special connotation of acceptance and esteem. Let the employees select their own candidates for best service employees, and then make the reward something really special.

Look for ways to recognize and reward your employees when they provide extraordinary service, and the dividends you reap will more than offset the cost involved.

CLOSING THE LOOP

To do what we've outlined in this book will require zeal, commitment, and an absolute dedication from the top people in your organization. Gaining the service advantage through superior customer knowledge will require intense scrutiny of the organization and all its systems.

Getting everyone's attention focused on the customer is a sizable undertaking, but one that is worth the effort in a competitive business environment. Each person, especially your managers, needs to learn your business's service strategy, that is, what you promise to your customers. Because the frontline manager and supervisor are the people who are going to make it happen for you. All managers and employees need to recognize the moments of truth that happen in your business, day in and day out. Every department must be trained to create a cycle of service to map out the critical moments of truth as they happen from the customer's perspective. And everyone needs to become conscious of service targets they can focus their improvement efforts upon and make happen.

You *can* teach people to deliver extraordinary service if they are willing and able. If they are able, have been carefully trained, but are still unwilling, then you have another kind of problem. You may have to ask yourself how long you can afford to keep an employee or manager who patently refuses to put your customers first.

Even with a carefully selected, oriented, and trained fighting force, the battle is not yet won. The fight for your customers' loyalty will never really end. In the decade ahead, and beyond, the winners in the service game will be those companies that make superior customer knowledge an integral part of their organizational culture.

It's the only way we know of to create a real difference in the minds of customers between your business and that of your competitors.

And that's the name of the game, isn't it?

NOTE

1. Carol Isaac Barden, "The Gadget King," *Profiles, Inc.*, March 1988, p. 69.

INDEX

A

Albrecht, Karl, 24, 94 n, 145,
    170 n, 207 n, 223
Alreck, Pamela L., 82 n, 108 n
American Banker, The, 25, 203
American Demographics, 98
Apocalypse Now, 57
At America's Service, 36, 78
Atlantic Monthly, 96
ATM; *see* Automated teller
    machines
Attribute matrix, 171–74
    illustrated, 175
    internal climate and, 178
    using survey data, 171
Attributes, prioritizing, 179–80
Automated teller machines (ATMs),
    65, 74

B

Baby boomers, 53, 56–60
    demand for undivided attention,
        59
    idealism of the 60s and, 57
    major value drives of, 57–59
    objections and, 60
    product choices, 60
    relationships and, 59
    resistance to external
        motivation, 60
Baby busters, 54
Back To The Future, 57

Bad news moment of truth, 47–48
    sensitivity and, 48
Balkcom, James, 9
Bank of America, 74
Barden, Carol Isaac, 217, 230 n
Barnum Communications of
    Chicago, 52
Barrier, John, 13
Barry Leeds & Associates, 32
Berry, Leonard, 25
Big, 54
Big Chill Generation at Work, 56,
    82 n
Big picture reports, 164–65
Bimodal split pattern, 164
Blueprint for excellence, 83–84
Bressler, Phil, 193, 204
Burns, Robert, 20
Business Month, 187, 207 n
Business Week, 187, 207 n
"Bus-rider syndrome, The," 37
Buy/no buy moment of truth, 42–44

C

Capture accounts, 6
Carlzon, Jan, 13, 30, 104–5, 108 n,
    174
Carney, Frank, 63
Chas. H. Stevens, 82
Chrysler Corporation, 203, 212
Cincinnati Gas and Electric
    Company (CG&E), 188

Citicorp, 10
Cleveland Clinic Foundation, 102
Club Mediteranee (Club Med),
    190–91
Coming Home, 57
Competitive strength zone, 176,
    178
Competitive vulnerability zone,
    175–76, 178
Computer-driven telephone
    systems, 74
Con artists, 2–4
    knowing the "mark," 2–3
    market research and, 3–4
Congruence, 41–42
Conjoint preference analysis, 173,
    179
Context-bound, 37
Cost containment
    constraint of, 25
    three-way pull and, 25–26
Credit cards, 65
Critical incidents, 121
Critical moments of truth, 34–36
    customer confidence and, 35–36
    customer satisfaction and, 35
Crouse, Lindsey, 2–3
Cultural difference
    customers, 62–63
    service employees, 62
Cultural drives among Americans
    acquiring material goods, 64
    buy now/pay later syndrome, 65
    taking action and, 63–64
    work hard/play hard syndrome,
        64–65
    young, good-looking and slim
        syndrome, 65–66
Customer
    alienation of, 16–18
    as an asset, 12–14
    attitudes, beliefs, and values,
        52–53
    and changeable moods, 115–16
    changing diets, 68
    definition of, 19–20
    depersonalization of, 15–16

Customer—(*continued*)
    discrete generational groups, 53
    mental and emotional states,
        113–15
    moment of truth and, 30–33
    in the 1990s, 52
    open season on, 4–5
    service quality perception, 75
    the service triangle and, 27
    thinking like the, 20–23
Customer as enemy context, 77–78
Customer Bill of Rights, 212–14
Customer complaints, managing,
    196–204
    aggressive customer and, 200
    chronic complainer, 202–4
    high roller customer, 201
    meek customer and, 199–200
    rip-off customer, 201–2
    survey of complaints, 199
Customer-driven organization, 82
Customer interviews; *see also*
    Focus group
    depth interviews, 120–21
    face to face advantage, 119–20
    intercept interviews, 121–23
    on-site interviews, 125
    opportunity interviews, 123–24
    process summary, 140–41
    telephone interviews, 124–25
Customer perception research,
    95–96
Customer report card
    business success and, 87–88
    customer wants and, 89–90
    explanation of, 84
    identifying what is on, 88–89
    key service quality attributes,
        84–86
    and meeting service
        requirements, 90
    sample of, 90–91
    score on service attributes, 87
    validating, 183–85
Customer service departments
    (CSD), 116–17

Customer Styles Model, 100–101, 104
Customer survey response, 192–93
Custometrics, 156
Custometrics Customer Satisfaction Survey System, 170 n
Cycle of service, 33–34
    illustrated, 34
    mapping out, 33
    moments of truth and, 33–34

D

Data-gathering instrument design, 189–92
    internal climate assessment and, 190
    service attribute matrix and, 189
Deer Hunter, The, 57
Delivering better, 216–19
    courier services and, 218
    face to face delivery, 218–19
    knowing customer wants, 217
    mail order houses and, 218
Demographic bias, 193–94
Demographics, 95–99, 149
    collecting data, 98–99
    explanation of, 96–97
    importance of, 97–98
Demographic variables, 164–65
Dent, Ron, 6, 145, 178
Denver Post, The, 49 n, 142 n, 207 n, 218–19
Digital Equipment Corporation (DEC), 187
Disneyland context, 75–76
Domino's Pizza, 193, 204, 210
Du Pont, 9

E

Early Majority, 103
Edison Electric Institute (EEI), 15
Employee link, 9–10
    case studies, 10–12
Employee report card, 92–93

Employees
    attracting and keeping the best, 223–24
    as customer advocates, 112–13
    customer contact and, 111–12
    evaluating, 227–29
    as frontline radar, 110–11
    orientation of, 225–26
    recognition and, 228–29
    selection process, 224–25
    training process, 226–27
Employee time accounts, 67
Explicit service promise, 210–12; *see also* Money back guarantees

F

Fast friends context, 77
Fax phenomenon, 73
Federal Express, 218
Final service criteria
    size of organization and, 180–81
    using survey results, 181–82
Fire House Car Wash, The, 10–11
First level customers, 88
Focus group, 90, 147, 148, 185, 189
    attribute analysis, 137–38
    case studies, 138–40
    conducting interviews, 131–34
    critical factors learned from, 127
    interocular impact and, 134
    interpreting results, 136–38
    interviewing, 125–26
    interview preparation, 130–31
    number and size of groups, 130
    questioning techniques, 134–35
    reason for using, 126–27
    recruiting the focus group, 127–29
Fortune, 23 n, 82 n, 142 n
Fourth level customers, 89
Frames of reference, 40–41, 51
Fraze, James, 23 n
Frequency table, 161
Frequent Flier, 82 n, 207 n

Full Metal Jacket, 57

G

Gallup Poll, 147
Galvin, Robert, 126
Geier, Hans, 229
General Motors (GM), 121
Goodstadt, Paul, 223–24
Graham, Lawrence, 82 n
Gray Zone, 177–78
*Great Expectations: America and
    the Baby Boom Generation,* 56,
    82 n
Greenberg, Peter, 23 n

H

Hamdan, Lawrence, 82 n
Hanks, Tom, 54
Heckert, Richard E., 9
High demand/high people
    orientation, 102
High demand/high process
    orientation, 101–2
High importance/high
    performance, 176
High importance/low performance,
    175–76
Hillkerk, John, 142 n, 207 n
Hilton Hotels, 69
Holiday Inn, 196–97
Home Shopping Club (HSC), 72–73
Hospitals, 207 n
House of Games, 2
Hultner, Wolfgang, 8

I

Iacocca, Lee, 203, 212
IBM, 170 n, 187
Imbert, Peter, Sir, 216–17
Implicit service promise, 209–10
Informal feedback, 194–96

*In Search of Excellence: Lessons
    from America's Best
    Companies,* 118 n
Internal climate assessment, 109
Internal customers, 33
    validating report card for, 185
Internal Revenue Service, 126
Internal Service Triangle, 36
Interocular impact test, 134, 164
Irrelevant superiority zone, 177
Ivie, Jerry, 7

J–K

Johnson, Roger, 50
Jones, Landon Y., 56, 82 n
Karl Albrecht's Service Triangle;
    see Service triangle
Kates, Dick, 10
Kennametal, Inc., 4, 30–31, 212
Key service attributes, 84–86, 171,
    189, 194; *see also* Focus group
King, Patricia, 82 n
King and I, The, 109
Knowing your customer
    buying patterns and motivations,
        5
    case studies, 5–9
    con artist and, 2–4
    as individuals, 5
    systematic approach to, 1

L

LaBella, Leonard, 100
Landers, Ann, 18
Landon, Alf, 147
Lands' End, 214–15
Late Majority, 103
Lauri, John, 189
Lee, John, 82
Leeds, Barry, 32
Likert, Rensis, 154
Likert scale, 154–55
Line graph prioritizing, 179

Literary Digest, 147
L.L. Bean, Inc., 214–16, 220
Low demand/people orientation,
    103–5
Low demand/process orientation,
    102–3
Low importance/low performance,
    176
Lucas, Claire, 11–12
Lucky's, 36

M

McCormick, John, 49
McKenna, Quentin, 4, 30, 212
Main, Jeremy, 74, 82 n
Management's personal radar,
    117–18
Management system, 28–29
"Managers on the Move" (MOM),
    117–18
Mandarin Oriental Hotel, The, 8
Mantegna, Joe, 2
Marketing News, 207 n
Market shift, 50
    changing values and, 50–52
Marriott, J. Willard "Bill," 6
Marriott Corporation, 6, 69,
    187–88
Mean value, 160, 165
Measurement habit, 187–88
Memmott, Mark, 23 n
Moment of truth model
    congruence and, 41
    explanation, 36–37
    illustrated, 37
Moments of truth, 30–32, 108 n
Money back guarantees, 214–16
Motorola, Inc., 8–9, 126
Mystery shoppers, 204–5

N

National Westminster Bank of
    London (Nat West), 223–24

Newmarket Hilton, 18
Newsweek, 32, 49 n, 82, 82 n
Nimeroff, Dinah, 10
*1989 Information Please Almanac,
    The,* 98
Nordstrom, Jim, 5
Nordstrom Company, 5–6, 112, 202,
    210
No response cases, 162
Northwestern Mutual Life
    Insurance Co., 120

O

Old National Bank, 13
Opinion surveys, 154
*Organization Development: A Total
    Systems Approach to Change in
    Any Business Organization,*
    94 n

P

Palais Royal, 7, 59, 195–96
Paudre Valley Hospital (PVH),
    96–97, 189
Peebles, 204–5
Peebles, W. S., III, 205
Perpetually recurring moment of
    truth, 48–49
Peters, Thomas J., 117, 118 n
Pete's Coney Island, 11
Phillips, Dorothy, 52
Pilot test, 156
Planes, Trains and Automobiles, 47
Platoon, 57
Plumb Creek Timber Co., 206
Pluralism, 51
Porter, Michael, 25
Portman Hotel, The, 69
Powell, Bill, 49
Press, Irwin, 203
Preteens, 54–55
Profiles Inc., 217, 230

Psychographics, 95, 149
  collecting data, 105–6
  explanation of, 99–100
  importance of, 100–101
Public Service Company of
  Colorado, 51, 128, 206–7

Q

Qualitative methods, 106–7
Quality of work life factors (QWL);
  see Employee report card
Quantitative methods, 107
Quill Corporation, 213–14

R

Raines, Claire, 53, 56, 82 n
Rand Youth Poll of 1984, 55
Recovering from mistakes, 219–20
Referral moment of truth, 46–47
  accentuating the negative and,
  46
Relative indifference zone, 176
Rent-A-Center, 63
Representative sample, 146–47
Repurchase decision, 45–46
Research methods, 106
Research model, 148
Research tools, 107–8
*Resource/American Society for
  Personnel Administration,* 23 n
Response sheets, 163–65
Richards, Geoffery, 73
Rocky Mountain News, 218
Roosevelt, Franklin, 147
Rosenstein, Jay, 25, 49, 49 n

S

Scandinavian Airlines System
  (SAS), 13, 30–31, 103–4
Schrello, Don, 192

Schuenke, Donald, 120
Scotland Yard, 216–17
Second level customers, 89
Seifert, Tom, 98
Sellers, Patricia, 23 n, 142 n
Selling better, 208–16
  explicit service promise, 210–12
  implicit service promise, 209–10
Service advantage summary,
  229–30
Service America! 24, 36, 223
*Service America: Doing Business In
  the New Economy,* 207 n
Service attribute matrix, 174–75,
  189
Service business and hunting
  analogy, 4
Service context, 37–40
  context-bound and, 37
  factors that contribute to, 39–40
Service contexts of the 1990s, 71
  automatic teller machines
  (ATMs), 74–75
  fax phenomenon, 73
  telephone contact with
  customers, 71–72
  television shopping, 72–73
Service driven organization, 187
Service employee's frame of
  reference, 41
Service management
  competition and, 24–26
  defined, 24
  model of, 25–26
  transformational concept and, 24
Service point average, 170–80
Service products of the 1990s, 66
  cruise lines and, 67–68
  health care customers and,
  70–71
  hotel customers and, 69–70
  restaurant customers and, 68–69
  travel industry and, 66–67
Service promise
  explanation of, 209
  market value of, 212–14

Service Quality Measurement
System (SQMS), 186–87
basic structure for, 189
producing usable reports, 205–7
using mystery shoppers, 204–5
Service subjects, 85; *see also* Key
service attributes
Service triangle, 26, 36
customer and, 27
defined, 26
people and, 28
service strategy, 27
systems and, 28
Service winners in 1990s, 81–89
Settle, Robert B., 82 n, 108 n
Seven sins of service, 78–81
Shared frame of reference, 21–22
Sharper Image, The, 217–18
Shaw, George Bernard, 20
Shrinking labor pool, 62
Simmons College Market Survey,
56
Sinding, Christian, 103, 174
Sir Francis Drake Hotel, 200
"Sixty Minutes," 72
The Society of Teachers of Family
Medicine (STFM), 221–23
Something for nothing; *see* Con
artists
Special moments of truth, 42
Sports Illustrated, 96
Standard deviation, 162
State Bank of South Australia, 6,
145, 178
Steamboard Ski Corporation, 229
Survey questionnaire, 148, 192–94
creating questions, 152–56
demographic and psychographic
data, 149
design problems, 150–51
finalizing, 157–58
pilot testing, 156–57
subgrouping respondents, 150
types of questions, 154

Survey reports
designing report for reader, 167
formatting, 166–69
importance of detail correctness,
169–70
Survey response bias, 151–52
guarding against, 193
key service attribute and, 194
reality check and, 193
Surveys
collecting data, 158–59
defining the research model, 148
five phases to, 143
insuring response, 192–93
measuring opinions with
numbers, 159–61
planning the project, 144–46
population size, 151–52
processing the data, 163
representative sampling and,
146–47
special subpopulations, 165–66
specifying business objectives,
144
and target population, 146
Survey statistics, 159
calculating averages, 160–61
frequency tables, 161–62
no response cases, 162
standard deviation, 162
using computer, 163
Systems
building better, 220–23
customer-friendly, 221
employee-friendly, 221
management, 28–29
model for assessing, 222
rules and regulations in, 29
social aspects of, 29–30
technical part of, 29

T

Taylor, Marilyn, 51
Technical Assistance Research
Programs, Inc., 199

Techsonic Industries, 9
Teenagers, 55–56
Television shopping, 72–73
Thalheimer, Richard, 217–18
Thielen, Gregory, 128
Third level customers, 89
"Thirtysomething," 57
Thomas, Gerald M., 18–19
"Three Card Monte," 3
Ticketmaster, 43
Time, 57
Tinsley, Elisa, 23 n
Toyota, 32
Traditionalists, 60–61
  and baby boomers compared, 61
  leisure time and, 61
Training, 82 n
Transformational concept, 24
Travelers Express Company (TE),
  191–92
Trigano, Gilbert, 191

U

Unconscious discrimination, 51
United Parcel Service, 218
United States Bureau of Census, 56
United States Postal Service, 218
USA Today, 23 n, 142 n, 207 n
U.S. News and World Report, 207 n

V

Valence, 173
Value for money moment of truth,
  44–45
View through the customer's eyes,
  21

W

Wagner, Dennis, 69, 187
Waterman, Robert H., 117, 118 n
Weighted average, 160
Wells Fargo, 74
Western Digital Corporation, 50
Westin Kauai Service Context,
  76–77
White Office of Consumer Affairs,
  The, 199
W. H. Smith Company, 196, 198
*Why They Buy: American
  Consumers Inside and Out,*
  82 n, 108 n
"The Wonder Years," 57

Y–Z

Yankelovich Monitor Service, 105
Young adults, 55–56
*Youth Trends: Capturing the $200
  Billion Youth Market,* 82 n
Zemke, Ron, 24, 82 n, 207 n
Zone of Indifference; *see* Gray Zone